Living in Mexico
Vivre au Mexique

Living in Mexico
Vivre au Mexique

Barbara & René Stoeltie

EDITED BY · HERAUSGEGEBEN VON · SOUS LA DIRECTION DE

Angelika Taschen

TASCHEN

KÖLN LONDON LOS ANGELES MADRID PARIS TOKYO

CONTENTS

INHALT

SOMMAIRE

Casa Luis Barragan

Colonia Tacubaya

Mexico City

After Luis Barragán's death two books were found lying unfinished on his bedside table: Emily Brontë's "Wuthering Heights" and André Maurois's "A la recherche de Marcel Proust". This only goes to show that the spirit of Romanticism was never far from the legendary Mexican architect's heart – and that Barragán's work, all too often described as cerebral and minimalist, sprang from a lyrical mind. This "poet of stone", born in Guadalajara in 1902, began his career at the age of 23, establishing himself as one of the figureheads of Mexico's new architectural movement. Barragán, who was greatly influenced by the beauty of Italian towns and the gardens of El Generalife in Granada, went on to create his own distinctive constructions, which were marked by the sobriety of their style and used a typical palette of colours (bright yellows, Mexican pinks, electric blues and virginal whites). Barragán also experimented with a subtle play on volume, transforming his creations into three-dimensional Constructivist artworks. The architect's Mexican home, built in 1948 and where he died in 1988, reflects his love of visual calm and perfect volumes.

The walls in the entrance hall have been restored to their original colour.

Die Mauern im Eingangsbereich wurden wieder in ihrer ursprünglichen Farbe gestrichen.

Dans l'entrée, les murs ont retrouvé leur teinte d'origine.

Nach seinem Tod fand man auf seinem Nachttisch zwei Bücher, die er gerade zu lesen begonnen hatte: »Sturmhöhe« von Emily Brontë und »Auf den Spuren von Marcel Proust« von André Maurois. Die Romantik schien dem großen Architekten Luis Barragán also nicht fremd zu sein und man kann vermuten, dass auch sein Werk, das allzu lange als intellektuell und minimalistisch galt, aus einer Gedankenwelt erwachsen ist, die lyrischen Empfindungen durchaus aufgeschlossen war. Dieser »Poet des Steins«, 1902 in Guadalajara geboren, wurde schon mit 23 Jahren zur Galionsfigur einer neuen Architektur. Die Schönheit italienischer Städte und die Gärten des Generalife in Granada beeinflussten Barrágans Werk, welches sich durch die Einfachheit der Konstruktionen auszeichnet. Sein subtiles Spiel mit Räumen und seine Farbpalette aus leuchtendem Gelb, Mexikanisch-Rosa, kräftigem Hellblau und Schneeweiß ließen seine Gebäude wie dreidimensionale konstruktivistische Gemälde erscheinen. Barragáns Streben nach einem ruhigen Erscheinungsbild und der Perfektion des Raumes spiegeln sich auch in seinem 1948 in Mexico City gebauten Privathaus, in dem er 1988 starb.

Après sa mort, on a trouvé sur sa table de chevet deux livres dont il venait de commencer la lecture: «Les Hauts de Hurlevent», d'Emily Brontë et «A la recherche de Marcel Proust», d'André Maurois. Ceci tend à prouver que le romantisme n'était pas étranger au grand architecte Luis Barragán et que son œuvre, trop longtemps décrite comme cérébrale et minimaliste, est née d'un esprit sensible aux accents lyriques. Ce poète de la pierre, né à Guadalajara en 1902, s'est manifesté dès ses débuts à 23 ans comme l'une des figures de proue d'une architecture nouvelle. Très influencé par la beauté des villes italiennes et par les jardins d'El Generalife à Grenade, Barragán s'est distingué par la sobriété de ses constructions, par sa palette de jaune vif, de rose mexicain, de bleu électrique et de blanc virginal et par ce jeu subtil de volumes qui transforment ses créations en tableaux constructivistes tridimensionnels. Sa maison privée à Mexico, construite en 1948 et où il est mort en 1988, reflète sa volonté de calme visuel et de perfection inégalée des volumes.

The garden's luxuriant
green foliage is caught
in the reflection of a
hand-blown glass vase
on the dining-room
window-sill.

*Auf der Fensterbank im
Esszimmer spiegelt sich
der üppige Garten in
einer Vase aus mundge-
blasenem Glas.*

*Dans la salle à manger,
un vase en verre soufflé,
posé sur l'appui de fenê-
tre, reflète l'image du
jardin luxuriant.*

*Secluded behind high
stone parapets, this
private terrace with its
vivid pink wall and
flamboyant cascades
of bougainvillea is a
magical sight.*

*Mit ihrer Wand in
leuchtendem Rosa und
den Kaskaden von Bou-
gainvillea bietet die
von hohen Mauern ge-
schützte Terrasse einen
bezaubernden Anblick.*

*Protégée par de hauts
murs, la terrasse en-
chante le regard avec
son mur rose vif et ses
cascades de bougainvil-
lées.*

RIGHT: *The entrance hall is stunning in its simplicity. A bare pink wall together with the pure lines of the staircase and simple furniture create an atmosphere of peace and calm.*
FOLLOWING PAGES: *The corridor leading to one of the bedrooms is painted yellow, complementing the sections of natural woodwork and plain, wood doors. The copy of a Josef Albers painting hung in the downstairs living room completes the pure, simple décor.*

RECHTS: *Der Eingangsraum überrascht: Die rosafarbene Wand, eine schlichte Treppe und streng geometrische Möbel schaffen ein ruhiges Ambiente.*
FOLGENDE DOPPEL-SEITE: *Der Gang, der zu einem der Zimmer führt, wurde gelb gestrichen, dazu passen die Täfelungen und Türen aus Naturholz. Im Erdgeschoss ergänzt die Kopie eines Gemäldes von Josef Albers die schnörkellose Einrichtung des Wohnzimmers.*

A DROITE: *Le hall d'entrée est surprenant. Un mur rose, un escalier épuré et des meubles aux lignes sévères créent une ambiance très calme.*
DOUBLE PAGE SUI-VANTE: *Le couloir qui mène vers une des chambres est peint en jaune avec des pans et des portes en bois naturel. Dans le séjour au rez-de-chaussée, la copie d'un tableau de Josef Albers complète la décoration dépouillée.*

ABOVE AND RIGHT:
In the vast space of the studio there is nothing to distract the eye from the beauty of line and volume. The architect has created a fireplace in the wall separating the entrance hall from the studio.
FACING PAGE: *Luis Barragán had an impeccable eye for colour and this is reflected throughout in immaculately painted walls, an interior shutter in Mexican pink, a ceiling punctuated with bright yellow beams and the furniture set off by pale wooden floorboards.*

OBEN UND RECHTS:
In dem geräumigen Studio lenkt nichts von der Geradlinigkeit des Raumes ab. Zwischen Eingangsbereich und Studio hat der Architekt einen Kamin in die Wand eingelassen.
RECHTE SEITE:
Luis Barragáns außergewöhnliches Gespür für Farbgestaltung zeigt sich in den sauber gestrichenen Wänden, den kräftig-gelben Balken der Zimmerdecke, dem mexikanisch-pinkfarbenen Fensterladen sowie den Möbeln und dem hellen Parkett.

CI-DESSUS ET A
DROITE: *Dans le vaste studio, rien ne distrait le regard de la beauté des volumes et des lignes. L'architecte a intégré une cheminée dans le mur qui sépare l'entrée du studio.*
PAGE DE DROITE:
Des murs immaculés, un plafond embelli par le rythme des poutres jaune vif, un volet intérieur rose mexicain, des meubles et un parquet blond témoignent des qualités exceptionnelles de coloriste de Luis Barragán.

FACING PAGE: *This narrow staircase leads down to the ground floor.*
RIGHT: *Luis Barragán's bedroom is a study in austerity, the only décor being a crucifix and a small collection of objets d'art that reflects the Mexican architect's pure, ascetic tastes.*

LINKE SEITE: *Die schmale Treppe führt ins Erdgeschoss.*
RECHTS: *Kruzifix und Kunstobjekte in Barragáns schlichtem Schlafzimmer zeugen von seinem puristischen Geschmack.*

PAGE DE GAUCHE: *L'étroit escalier mène au rez-de-chaussée.*
A DROITE: *Dans la chambre de Barragán, dépouillée à l'extrême, le crucifix et les objets d'art témoignent de la rigueur chère à l'architecte.*

A CONVERTED CHAPEL

Sergio Berger

Mexico City

Sergio Berger is young, handsome and at the height of profes-
sional success after opening "Ivory", his third restaurant in the
Mexican capital. Despite his lightning rise to fame, Sergio has
retained the natural modesty and timidity common to romantic
souls such as himself. These aspects of the restaurant owner's
character led him to make a rather unusual choice of home,
setting himself up in a 16th-century chapel. But Sergio never
had any intention of living in a shrine, surrounded by burning
candles and the reproving stares of plaster saints. While the
chapel's original frescoes and Baroque Hispanic altar with its
ornate gilt surrounds have been retained, this historical décor
starkly contrasts with the modern minimalist architecture and
the owner's eclectic tastes. His collection of contemporary art,
African artworks and an impressive variety of furniture sets
up an interesting visual tension between itself and the religious
surroundings. In short, Sergio Berger brings 21st-century style
and a sense of fun to chapel life!

*A brightly coloured
budgerigar; detail of
a painting by Ray
Smith.*

*Ein hübscher Wellen-
sittich, Ausschnitt aus
einem Gemälde von
Ray Smith.*

*Une jolie perruche,
détail d'un tableau
signé Ray Smith.*

Er ist jung und gut aussehend und hat gerade mit »Ivory« sein drittes Restaurant in der mexikanischen Hauptstadt eröffnet. Dabei hat sich Sergio Berger trotz seines blendenden Erfolgs die Bescheidenheit und Zurückhaltung eines sensiblen Naturells bewahrt. Für diesen Charakterzug spricht auch die ungewöhnliche Entscheidung, sich in einer Kapelle aus dem 16. Jahrhundert einzurichten. Allerdings stand ihm nicht der Sinn danach, seine Tage in einer Leichenhalle zu verbringen, umringt von Kerzen und farbigen Heiligenfiguren aus Gips, die ihn missbilligend anblicken könnten. Deshalb ließ der Junggastronom nur den reich verzierten und vergoldeten hispanischen Barockaltar sowie die Fresken unangetastet. Der Kontrast von historischen Dekorationen, karger Architektur und Sergios eklektizistischem Geschmack, in dem zeitgenössische und afrikanische Kunst sich mit Möbeln aller Stilrichtungen verbinden, lässt natürlich eine große visuelle Spannung entstehen. In einer Kapelle leben, ja, aber mit der Einstellung des 21. Jahrhunderts und ohne sich dabei allzu ernst zu nehmen.

Tucked away in the heart of town, this tranquil enclave with its centuries-old walled gardens stands as an ode to rural life.

Diese mitten in der Stadt gelegene, friedliche Enklave mit ihren jahrhundertealten, ummauerten Gärten wirkt wie der Inbegriff ländlichen Lebens.

Au cœur de la ville, cette enclave paisible avec ses jardins murés vieux de plusieurs siècles fait l'éloge de la vie rurale.

Il est jeune et beau et vient d'ouvrir son troisième restaurant baptisé «Ivory» dans la capitale mexicaine. En dépit de son succès foudroyant, Sergio Berger a su préserver une modestie et une timidité qui sont le propre des êtres romantiques. D'ailleurs, son choix singulier de s'installer dans une chapelle du 16e siècle , ne fait qu'accentuer cet aspect de son caractère. Néanmoins, Sergio n'avait aucune envie de passer ses journées dans une ambiance de chapelle ardente, entouré de cierges et de saints en plâtre polychrome déplorant son intrusion et le fixant d'un air réprobateur. Le jeune restaurateur a gardé l'autel hispanique baroque lourdement doré et ornementé et n'a pas touché aux fresques. Le contraste entre les décorations d'époque, l'architecture sévère et le goût éclectique de Sergio qui combine l'art contemporain, l'art africain et les meubles en tout genre, crée bien sûr une grande tension visuelle. D'accord pour vivre dans une chapelle, mais dans l'esprit du 21e siècle et sans trop se prendre au sérieux.

The vivid colours of Ray Smith's painting blend with the kaleidoscopic assortment of furniture in the living room (converted from its former existence as a chapel).

Im Wohnzimmer, der früheren Kapelle, passt das farbenfrohe Gemälde von Ray Smith perfekt zu den Möbeln der unterschiedlichen Stilrichtungen.

Le tableau aux vives couleurs de Ray Smith se marie avec bonheur aux meubles hétéroclites dans le séjour, une ancienne chapelle.

LEFT AND FACING PAGE: *Sergio has created a guest room in the mezzanine complete with an inviting couch piled high with Indian cushions. The hand of Buddha is carved out of wood.*
PAGE 26: *Sergio retained the delicate frescoes adorning the chapel walls.*
PAGE 27: *An antique wooden reredos, hand-painted and embellished with exquisite gilt decoration, is the central feature in the living room.*

LINKS UND RECHTE SEITE: *Im Zwischengeschoss hat Sergio ein Gästezimmer mit einem Sofa eingerichtet, auf dem mehrere aus Indien mitgebrachte Kissen liegen. Die Hand des Buddha ist aus Holz.*
SEITE 26: *Den zarten Freskenschmuck der Kapelle hat Sergio erhalten.*
SEITE 27: *Den Blickfang im Wohnzimmer bildet die historische Altarrückwand aus bemaltem und vergoldetem Holz.*

A GAUCHE ET PAGE DE DROITE: *Sergio a créé une chambre d'amis dans l'entresol en y installant un lit de repos dissimulé sous un amoncellement de coussins rapportés d'Inde. La main de Bouddha est en bois sculpté.*
PAGE 26: *Sergio a conservé les fresques délicates qui ornent les murs de la chapelle.*
PAGE 27: *L'ancien retable en bois peint et doré domine le séjour.*

A VILLAGE HOUSE

Morelos

Secluded behind a thick pink-ochre coloured wall and shielded
by a massive front door designed to keep out the most prying
of eyes, it's clear that those who retreat here are determined to
cut themselves off from the world. No need for a "beware of
the dog" sign! If the owners grant you admittance to their inner
sanctum, a servant will show you through to a high, light-filled
living room where sofas and armchairs are tastefully arranged.
Design highlights such as the pale blue-beamed ceiling and
beautiful antique furniture reflect the exquisite taste and decor-
ating skills of the masters of the house. Wandering through the
cool, calm and spacious interiors, visitors will be impressed by
the dining room where the eye is instantly caught by an 18th-
century Japanese screen, a solid refectory table and a wooden
sculpture of a horse. The bedroom, a masterpiece of sober,
understated beauty, houses a magnificent Aztec statue fash-
ioned out of terracotta. But the garden is the real star of the
show, its riot of tropical vegetation dotted with vivid splashes
of bougainvillea.

PREVIOUS PAGES:
*the pool surrounded by
bougainvillea.*
LEFT: *one of the patios
at the bottom of the
garden.*
ABOVE: *The leaf of a
tropical plant shimmers
in the sunlight.*

**VORHERGEHENDE
DOPPELSEITE:** *Rings
um den Swimmingpool
blühen Bougainvilleen.*
LINKS: *Blick in einen
der Patios im hinteren
Teil des Gartens.*
OBEN: *Sonnenstrahlen
streifen das Blatt einer
tropischen Pflanze.*

**DOUBLE PAGE PRE-
CEDENTE:** *la piscine et
ses bougainvillées.*
A GAUCHE: *un des pa-
tios au fond du jardin.*
CI-DESSUS: *Le soleil
caresse la feuille d'une
plante tropicale.*

Die versteckte Lage hinter einer dicken rötlich-ockerfarbenen Mauer und die massive Tür, die vor neugierigen Blicken schützt, verraten schon das Bedürfnis der Bewohner, sich hier für ein Wochenende oder länger aus der Welt zurückzuziehen. Ein Schild nach dem Muster »Bissiger Hund« wird man jedoch vergeblich suchen. Wen die Besitzer hereinbitten, führt ein Dienstbote in einen hohen, hellen Salon mit makellosen Sofas und Sesseln. Die Decke mit blassblauen Balken und die stilvollen alten Möbel lassen den erlesenen Geschmack und das bemerkenswerte gestalterische Talent der Hausherren erkennen. In diesem weitläufigen und angenehm kühlen Haus genießt man gern die Annehmlichkeiten eines Esszimmers, in dem ein japanischer Wandschirm aus dem 18. Jahrhundert, eine solide Klostertafel und ein geschnitztes Holzpferd die Akzente setzen, oder die schlichte Schönheit eines Schlafraums, in dem eine wunderschöne aztekische Terrakottastatue thront. Der Garten mit seinen Bougainvillea in kräftigen Farben und seiner üppigen Tropenvegetation stellt jedoch selbst diese Innenräume in den Schatten.

Le fait qu'elle soit dissimulée derrière un mur épais couleur d'ocre rose et d'une porte massive qui décourage le regard des curieux trahit déjà l'attitude des habitants qui désirent se retirer du monde le temps d'un week-end ou davantage. Ici cependant pas d'écriteau du genre «chien méchant». Si les propriétaires daignent vous recevoir, le valet vous guidera vers un salon haut et clair dans lequel des canapés et des fauteuils immaculés vous accueilleront. Le plafond à poutres bleu pâle et de très beaux meubles anciens révèlent que les maîtres des lieux ont un goût exquis et un don remarquable pour la décoration. Dans cette vaste maison calme et fraîche, on se laisse facilement séduire par une salle à manger que dominent un paravent japonais 18e, une robuste table de réfectoire et un cheval en bois sculpté. Ou par la sobre beauté d'une chambre à coucher dans laquelle trône une magnifique statue aztèque en terre cuite. Mais le jardin vole la vedette aux espaces intérieurs avec ses bougainvillées aux vives couleurs et sa végétation tropicale exubérante.

This corridor, covered by a protective awning, leads to the bedrooms housed in the outbuildings.

Ein mit einem Wetterdach gedeckter Gang führt zu den Gebäuden, in denen die Schlafzimmer liegen.

Un corridor couvert d'un auvent mène aux bâtiments qui abritent les chambres à coucher.

CASA DE LEON

Evelyn Lambert

Cuernavaca

With her large-framed glasses and hair pulled back into a neat platinum chignon, Evelyn Lambert appeared to have discovered the secret of eternal youth. At the age of 97, she was still fired by remarkable energy and a tireless curiosity about the world around her and took a keen interest in the arts, especially 20th-century art, which she had admired, defended and collected with the passion of a true connoisseur. Evelyn, American by birth, discovered art through direct contact with artists themselves and she spent much of her life mixing with the greatest of them. Her refined sense of aesthetics led her to live in a splendid villa in Veneto before she settled in the heart of Cuernavaca in this magnificent 17th-century house in the late 1980s. These days the Casa de Leon, a former brothel known as the Casa del Gato (House of the Cat), still houses a superb collection of paintings, sculptures, antiques and objets d'art arranged according to Evelyn's original eye for décor. Sadly, the mistress of the Casa de Leon has passed away, leaving behind a wide circle of friends and admirers.

PREVIOUS PAGES: *The garden of the Casa de Leon is an oasis of greenery, its tranquillity broken only by birdsong and the gentle play of fountains.*
LEFT: *a detail of the traditional tilework lining the interior of the fireplace in the living room.*

VORHERGEHENDE DOPPELSEITE: *Der Garten der Casa de Leon ist eine grüne Oase, in der nur das Plätschern der Springbrunnen und die Vögel zu hören sind.*
LINKS: *Detail der traditionellen Fliesen, mit denen die Rückwand des Wohnzimmerkamins gekachelt wurde.*

DOUBLE PAGE PRECEDENTE: *Le jardin de la Casa de Leon est une oasis de verdure où l'on n'entend que le murmure des fontaines et le chant des oiseaux.*
A GAUCHE: *un détail des carreaux traditionnels qui tapissent le fond de la cheminée du séjour.*

Evelyn Lambert schien dem Geheimnis ewiger Jugend auf die Spur gekommen zu sein: Noch mit 97 Jahren legte sie eine beachtliche Energie an den Tag und verfolgte mit großem Interesse und Neugier das Geschehen auf dieser Welt, insbesondere in Bezug auf die Kunst. Mit Leidenschaft unterstützte und sammelte sie die von ihr bewunderte Kunst des 20. Jahrhunderts. Die gebürtige Amerikanerin, die eine riesige Brille und einen kleinen platinfarbenen Haarknoten trug, war über die Künstler zur Kunst gestoßen. Man konnte sie nur bewundern, diese Frau, die mit den Großen Umgang hatte und aus Liebe zum Schönen beschloss, sich in einer prächtigen Villa im Veneto niederzulassen, ehe sie Ende der 1980er Jahre in ein wunderbares Haus im Herzen von Cuernavaca zog. Die Casa de Leon, die einmal Casa del Gato (Haus der Katze) hieß und als Bordell diente, beherbergt heute immer noch Gemälde, Skulpturen, Objekte und Antiquitäten, allesamt mit einer Originalität angeordnet, die von Evelyns Talent zum Inszenieren zeugt. Mit fast 100 Jahren ist die Hausherrin nun verstorben. Sie verstand bis zuletzt ihre Freunde und Bewunderer zu bezaubern.

The mantelpiece showcases a terracotta jug by Picasso and a wood carving of a bird that Evelyn found in Maine.

Auf dem Kaminsims stehen ein Terrakottakrug von Picasso und eine Vogelskulptur aus Holz, die Evelyn in Maine aufgestöbert hat.

Sur la tablette de la cheminée une cruche en terre cuite de Picasso accompagne un oiseau en bois sculpté, déniché par Evelyn dans le Maine.

Evelyn Lambert semblait avoir découvert le secret de la jeunesse éternelle! A 97 ans, elle faisait encore preuve d'une énergie remarquable et d'une curiosité inlassable pour tout ce qui existe et surtout les arts. En particulier l'art du 20ᵉ siècle qu'elle n'a jamais cessé d'admirer, de défendre et de collectionner avec passion. Américaine de naissance, Evelyn, immenses lunettes et petit chignon platine, avait découvert l'art à travers les artistes. Impossible de ne pas admirer cette femme qui côtoyait les grands et qui choisit, par amour du beau, de vivre dans une superbe villa du Veneto, avant de s'installer à la fin des années 1980 dans une magnifique demeure du 17ᵉ siècle au cœur de Cuernavaca. Aujourd'hui la Casa de Leon, qui s'appelait jadis la Casa del Gato (la maison du chat) et était une maison close, abrite toujours les tableaux, les sculptures, les objets et les antiquités disposés avec une originalité qui révèle le talent d'Evelyn pour la mise en scène. Hélas, à l'approche de ses cent printemps, la maîtresse des lieux s'est éteinte. Mais elle continue toujours d'enchanter ses amis et ses admirateurs.

The painting by Jeremy Moon, "Indian Journey", offsets the colourful tones of a carved wooden fruit bowl.

Das Gemälde von Jeremy Moon, »Indian Journey«, passt sehr schön zu einer bunten Fruchtschale aus geschnitztem Holz.

Le tableau signé Jeremy Moon, «Indian Journey», s'harmonise avec une coupe à fruits en bois sculpté polychrome.

ABOVE AND FACING PAGE: *An elegant fountain, inspired by those found in Italian Renaissance gardens, supplies water to the swimming pool in the lower half of the garden. Standing by the fountain's basin, visitors have a stunning view of the garden and its lush vegetation.*
RIGHT: *A sculpture by Garth Evans from 1968 dominates the stairwell decorated with eye-catching mosaics and the gentle curve of a banister.*

OBEN UND RECHTE SEITE: *Das im unteren Teil des Gartens gelegene Schwimmbecken wird von einer eleganten Fontäne gespeist, die den Brunnen italienischer Renaissancegärten nachempfunden ist. Vom Brunnenbecken aus eröffnet sich eine wunderbare Aussicht auf den üppig wuchernden Garten.*
RECHTS: *Eine Garth-Evans-Skulptur von 1968 beherrscht das Treppenhaus mit seinen Mosaiken und dem sanft geschwungenen Handlauf.*

CI-DESSUS ET PAGE DE DROITE: *La piscine, située dans la partie basse du jardin, est alimentée en eau par une fontaine élégante inspirée de celles des jardins de la Renaissance italienne. Du bassin de la fontaine, on a une vue magnifique sur le jardin luxuriant.*
A DROITE: *Une sculpture signée Garth Evans, de 1968, domine la cage d'escalier avec ses mosaïques et sa rampe aux lignes souples.*

FACING PAGE: *Gifted with exceptional aesthetic taste and a "sense of the dramatic", Evelyn Lambert had transferred the décor of her now legendary Italian villa near Vicenza to her Mexican home in Cuernavaca. Francis Celentano's 1963 painting above the sofa, entitled "December 30", hangs alongside Venetian Blackamoors.*

RIGHT: *The hand-painted wooden wardrobe in the loggia is a masterpiece of Italian Renaissance cabinetwork.*

LINKE SEITE: *Mit ihrem ausgeprägten Sinn für »Dramatik« übertrug Evelyn die berühmte Einrichtung ihrer bei Vicenza gelegenen italienischen Villa in ihr mexikanisches Haus. Das Bild über dem Sofa mit dem Titel »December 30« hat Francis Celentano 1963 gemalt. Hier wird es kombiniert mit venezianischen Mohrenfigur-Leuchtern.*

RECHTS: *Der bemalte Holzschrank der Loggia ist ein Stück Tischlerkunst aus der italienischen Renaissance.*

PAGE DE GAUCHE: *Avec son sens exceptionnel du «dramatique», Evelyn transposait la décoration désormais célèbre de sa villa italienne située près de Vicence dans sa maison mexicaine. Le tableau au-dessus du canapé date de 1963. Il est signé Francis Celentano et s'intitule «December 30». Il côtoie ici des Blackamoors vénitiens.*

A DROITE: *L'armoire en bois peint de la loggia est un chef-d'œuvre d'ébénisterie de la Renaissance italienne.*

Casa de la Torre

Museo Robert Brady

Cuernavaca

In February 1990, the doors of number 4, Calle Netzahualcóy-otl in Cuernavaca swung open to the public, admitting them to the home of the American artist Robert Brady (1928–1986). Brady, born in Iowa to well-off parents who owned their own transport company, developed a passion for the arts at an early age. After studying at The Art Institute of Chicago and the Barnes Foundation in Philadelphia, he left America and moved to Europe, where he settled in Venice. Here he lived in the palace once occupied by the famous Italian artist Filippo de Pisis. This was conveniently located round the corner from Peggy Guggenheim, who was to become Brady's best friend and mentor. Fascinated by Mexico and the country's abundant art, colours and folklore, Brady moved to Cuernavaca and set up home in the Casa de la Torre in 1961. Over the ensuing decades Brady received royalty, diplomats, artists and the international jet set and transformed the house, once part of a Franciscan convent, into a labyrinth of elegant salons, each decorated with remarkable taste and filled with unique collections.

PREVIOUS PAGES: *Pots of sansevieria are ranged along the stone balustrade of Robert Brady's last home, silent sentries standing guard over the front door.*
LEFT: *detail of a bedroom alcove. The garland is made out of staff embellished with gold-leaf.*

VORHERGEHENDE DOPPELSEITE: *Auf der Brüstung der Stein-balustrade vorm Haus des verstorbenen Robert Brady reihen sich die eingetopften Sansevie-rien.*
LINKS: *Detailansicht einer Nische im Schlaf-zimmer, die eine mit Blattgold belegte Gir-lande aus Gipsfaser schmückt.*

DOUBLE PAGE PRE-CEDENTE: *Sur l'appui de la balustrade en pierre de la maison du regretté Robert Brady, des sansevières en pots sont alignées somme des sentinelles muettes.*
A GAUCHE: *détail d'une niche dans la chambre à coucher or-née d'une guirlande en staff dorée à la feuille.*

Im Februar 1990 öffneten sich die Türen des in der Calle Netzahualcóyotl Nr. 4 gelegenen Hauses in Cuernavaca, sodass die neugierige Öffentlichkeit sich ein Bild von der Wohnung des amerikanischen Malers Robert Brady (1928–1986) machen konnte. Brady, Sohn aus einer wohlhabenden Transportunternehmerfamilie, stammte aus Iowa. Er fühlte sich schon früh zur Kunst hingezogen. Nach dem Studium am Art Institute of Chicago und in der Barnes Foundation in Philadelphia verließ er seine Heimat und zog nach Europa, genauer gesagt, nach Venedig. Dort lebte er im Palast des berühmten Malers Filippo de Pisis, angenehmerweise ganz in der Nähe von Peggy Guggenheim, die zu seiner besten Freundin und Mentorin wurde. 1961, als ihn die Kunst, die Farben und die Folklore Mexikos faszinierten, bezog er die Casa de la Torre in Cuernavaca, die einst zu einem Franziskanerkloster gehört hatte. In den folgenden Jahrzehnten empfing Brady Diplomaten, Könige, Künstler und den internationalen Jet Set. Und er verwandelte das Haus in ein Labyrinth von eleganten Salons, die er mit bemerkenswertem Geschmack dekorierte und in denen er seine Sammlungen unterbrachte.

RIGHT: *the staircase leading to the kitchen and the dining room.*
PAGE 46: *A pre-Columbian statue strikes a meditative pose in the window.*

RECHTS: *die Steintreppe, die zu Küche und Esszimmer führt.*
SEITE 46: *Die präkolumbianische Statue in der Fensterlaibung scheint in der Sonne zu meditieren.*

A DROITE: *l'escalier qui mène à la cuisine et à la salle à manger.*
PAGE 46: *Une statue précolombienne semble méditer au soleil dans l'embrasure d'une fenêtre.*

En février 1990, les portes de la maison sise au 4 de la Calle Netzahualcóyotl à Cuernavaca se sont ouvertes, et les curieux ont pu visiter la demeure du peintre américain Robert Brady (1928–1986). Né dans le Iowa, au sein d'une famille aisée propriétaire d'une compagnie de transports, Brady fut attiré par les arts dès son plus jeune âge. Après des études à l'Art Institute of Chicago et à la Barnes Foundation de Philadelphie, il quitta son pays pour s'établir en Europe, à Venise plus précisément, dans le palais du célèbre peintre Filippo de Pisis, et agréablement proche de Peggy Guggenheim qui devint sa meilleure amie et son inspiratrice. En 1961, attiré par le Mexique, son art, ses couleurs et son folklore, il s'installa à Cuernavaca dans la Casa de la Torre qui faisait jadis partie du couvent franciscain. Durant les décennies qui suivirent, il accueillit des diplomates, des rois, des artistes et des membres de la jet-set, et transforma l'habitation en un dédale de salons élégants, décorés avec un goût remarquable et abritant des collections uniques.

The pool is surrounded by a high wall covered in a carpet of lush greenery.

Der Swimmingpool ist von einer hohen, begrünten Mauer umgeben.

La piscine est entourée d'un haut mur couvert de végétation.

PAGE 47: *The balcony of Brady's studio looks out onto the ancient convent with its imposing tower and stairways.*
FACING PAGE: *As a painter, Brady was sensitive to the charms of Mexican arts and craft. This bathroom is resplendent with traditional tilework.*
ABOVE: *The walls of this room are decorated with eye-catching masks. The bouquet of flowers was crocheted by Brady's cook.*
RIGHT: *In the bathroom, a gilt Buddha figure occupies a niche with a Moorish arch.*

SEITE 47: *Blick von Bradys Atelierbalkon auf Turm und Treppe des früheren Klosters.*
LINKE SEITE: *Der Maler liebte die mexikanische Volks- und Handwerkskunst. Das Badezimmer ist mit traditionellen Kacheln ausgestattet.*
OBEN: *Dieser Gewölbesaal ist mit außergewöhnlichen Masken dekoriert. Der Blumenstrauß ist eine Häkelarbeit von Bradys Köchin.*
RECHTS: *Im Badezimmer steht ein vergoldeter Buddha in einer Nische mit maurischen Bögen.*

PAGE 47: *Du balcon de l'atelier de Brady, on peut admirer la tour et les escaliers de l'ancien couvent.*
PAGE DE GAUCHE: *Le peintre était très sensible au folklore et à l'artisanat mexicains. Carreaux traditionnels dans cette salle de bains.*
CI-DESSUS: *Cette salle voûté est décorée de masques étonnants. Le bouquet de fleurs est un ouvrage au crochet réalisé par la cuisinière de Brady.*
A DROITE: *Dans la salle de bains aux arches mauresques un bouddha se dresse dans une niche.*

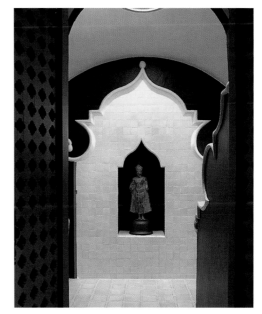

In this room, one of
the upstairs bedrooms,
Brady assembled an
audacious mix of styles,
juxtaposing Venetian
Baroque with the splen-
dours of India and the
Moorish influences of
Marrakesh. A bedroom
that doubles as a work
of art!

In einem der Zimmer
im Obergeschoss hat
Brady mutig die unter-
schiedlichsten Stile
zusammengebracht:
venezianisches Barock,
reich verzierte Objekte
aus Indien und mauri-
sche Akzente im Marra-
kesch-Stil. Das Ergebnis
kann sich sehen lassen.

Dans une des chambres
à l'étage, Brady a marié
avec une belle audace
les styles les plus divers:
baroque vénitien, splen-
deurs de l'Inde et ac-
cents mauresques style
Marrakech. Le résultat
est prodigieux.

VICTOR MANUEL CONTRERAS

Cuernavaca

Victor Manuel Contreras is known locally as "maestro", a mark of respect accorded to those who have achieved perfection in their chosen art, discipline or profession. Contreras's sculpting skills have earned him many honorary titles and commissions and his work graces numerous public squares and forecourts of official buildings in his homeland. The master's studio and eye-catching home make the perfect showcase for his creations past and present and work of all shapes and sizes is exhibited alongside classical statues and the work of sculptors he admires. With an eye for theatrical effect, Contreras has filled his spacious salons with paintings by Tamara de Lempicka (with whom he enjoyed a long "loving friendship") and the personal mementoes of Prince Youssoupov, who considered him as "a son fallen from heaven". This respected artist and talented storyteller honours Cuernavaca with his charismatic presence and enriches "the town of eternal spring" with a magnificent home and artist's studio destined to become a museum one day.

This antique statue, enshrined in an alcove just off the main staircase, is a fitting testimony to the beauty of Aztec art.

In einer Nische seitlich der großen Treppe zeugt eine uralte Statue von der Schönheit der aztekischen Kunst.

Dans une niche près du grand escalier, une statue très ancienne témoigne de la beauté de l'art aztèque.

Hier nennen ihn alle »Maestro« und dieser schmeichelhafte Titel, der anzeigt, dass jemand sein Fach, eine Kunst oder ein Handwerk vollendet beherrscht, zeugt vom Respekt, der Victor Manuel Contreras entgegengebracht wird. Seine Meisterschaft in der Bildhauerei hat ihm einige Ehrentitel und mehr als einen Auftrag eingebracht. Auf berühmten Plätzen und vor den Amtsgebäuden seines Landes stehen seine Werke. Das Atelier des Künstlers und die prächtige Wohnung bilden den geeigneten Rahmen für frühere und aktuelle Werke, die er zusammen mit klassischen Statuen oder Arbeiten von geschätzten Bildhauern arrangiert. Dem Theatralischen nicht abgeneigt, schmückt er seine weitläufigen Salons mit Gemälden von Tamara de Lempicka, mit der ihn lange eine »verliebte Freundschaft« verband, sowie mit persönlichen Erinnerungen an den Fürsten Jussupow, der ihn den »vom Himmel gefallenen Sohn« nannte. Der Hausherr, nicht nur ein geachteter Künstler, sondern auch ein talentierter Erzähler, beehrt Cuernavaca mit seiner charismatischen Erscheinung und bereichert »die Stadt des ewigen Frühlings« mit einem Wohnhaus und einem Atelier, die wohl eines Tages zum Museum werden.

Tout le monde l'appelle «maestro», et ce titre ronronnant qui indique la perfection dans une discipline, un art ou un métier, enveloppe Victor Manuel Contreras comme une belle cape de velours noir. Il faut dire que sa maîtrise de la sculpture lui a valu maints titres honorifiques, plus d'une commande et des places d'honneur sur les places et devant les bâtiments officiels de son pays. Dans son atelier comme dans sa superbe habitation, le maître expose ses créations d'hier et d'aujourd'hui en disposant ses œuvres de toutes tailles à côté de statues classiques ou d'œuvres de sculpteurs qu'il admire. Avec un penchant pour l'effet théâtral, il décore ses vastes salons avec des toiles de Tamara de Lempicka à qui le lia longtemps une «amitié amoureuse» et des souvenirs personnels du prince Youssoupov qui le surnomma «le fils tombé du ciel». Conteur de talent, artiste respecté, le maître des lieux honore Cuernavaca de sa présence charismatique et enrichit «la ville du printemps éternel» d'une demeure et d'un atelier qui seront un jour un musée.

The spacious landing of the main entrance has been transformed into a stage on which the owner of the house has imagined a grandiose décor of sturdy wooden benches, 19th-century bronze lamps, a turn-of-the-century table and the copy of an antique statue straight out of Pompeii.

Der große Treppenabsatz des Haupteingangs wurde gekonnt ausgestattet. Der Hausherr weiß, wie man mit soliden Sitzbänken, Bronzeleuchten aus dem 19. Jahrhundert, einem Tisch der Jahrhundertwende und der Replik einer antiken Statue aus Pompeji die größtmögliche Wirkung erzielt.

Le grand palier de l'entrée principale a été décoré avec un sens inné du spectacle. Le maître de maison sait tirer le maximum des banquettes robustes, de quelques luminaires en bronze 19ᵉ, d'une table fin de siècle et de la copie d'une statue antique digne de Pompéi.

Victor Manuel Contreras has also proved to be a master in the art of flower arranging.

Victor Manuel Contreras ist auch ein Meister in der Kunst des Blumenarrangements.

Victor Manuel Contreras est aussi passé maître dans l'art de composer les bouquets.

Under the guiding hand
of an architect, the
owner of this sumptuous
residence has infused his
home with Hollywood
glamour. The impressive
collection of artworks
and classical furniture,
not to mention the
monumental fireplace
in the main room, make
this a home fit for a star!

Mithilfe eines Architek-
ten hat der Hausherr
eine Wohnwelt im Stil
Hollywoods eingerich-
tet. Die Kunstwerke,
das klassische Mobiliar
und der prächtige, mo-
numentale Kamin sind
dem Domizil eines
Filmstars ebenbürtig.

Avec l'aide d'un archi-
tecte, le maître de mai-
son a aménagé une
demeure dans l'esprit
hollywoodien. Les œu-
vres d'art, le mobilier
classique et la superbe
cheminée monumentale
sont dignes de la pro-
priété d'une star.

$\mathcal{A}$ COLLECTOR'S PASSION

Manolo Rivero Cervera

Mérida

Manolo Rivero Cervera adopted the British expression "living above the shop" when it came to setting up his apartment above the Hotel Trinidad and his gallery. Rivero, who thus combines work and private life with the greatest of ease, is fired by a veritable passion for contemporary art. And he has proved his own talents as an artist and creator, putting together the most eclectic collection of paintings, furniture and objets d'art without ever committing the sin of bad taste or kitsch. Manolo's home is not recommended to those insensitive to the 20th-century charms of Pop Art, Op Art, Hyper-Realism and Surrealism, nor to those whose aesthetic senses may be shocked by the daring juxtaposition of a 'rocaille' sofa and scattering of Versace cushions with an Art Nouveau statuette and the lurid tones of a contemporary canvas. Just for the record, Julian Schnabel swears by Rivero's tastes and a New York gallery will soon stage an exhibit of his work. Meanwhile, guests at the Hotel Trinidad are enchanted by the magical atmosphere of this Aladdin's cave.

PREVIOUS PAGES: *The terrace is filled with paintings by contemporary artists and an eclectic collection of garden furniture, overhung by leafy green plants.*
LEFT: *Enshrined in a corner alcove, this carved wooden saint is decorated with a gilded crown and bedecked with antique rosary beads.*

VORHERGEHENDE DOPPELSEITE: *Auf der Terrasse mischen sich zeitgenössische Gemälde, Gartenmöbel verschiedener Art und Grünpflanzen.*
LINKS: *Die in einer Nische ausgestellte Heiligenfigur aus Holz erhielt eine goldene Krone und wurde mit alten Rosenkränzen geschmückt.*

DOUBLE PAGE PRECEDENTE: *La terrasse abrite des tableaux d'artistes contemporains, des meubles de jardin hétéroclites et des plantes vertes.*
A GAUCHE: *Une sainte en bois sculpté, exposée dans une niche, est coiffée d'une couronne dorée et décorée avec des chapelets anciens.*

»Living about the shop« – dieser typisch englische Ausdruck passt auf Manolo Rivero Cervera, der sich über seinem Hotel Trinidad und seiner Galerie eine Wohnung eingerichtet hat und Berufs- und Privatleben problemlos in Einklang bringt. Es ist schon beeindruckend, wie leidenschaftlich Rivero sich für die zeitgenössische Kunst interessiert, was für ein Talent als Künstler und Gestalter er entfaltet und mit welch sicherer Hand er die verschiedensten Objekte, Möbel und Gemälde kombiniert, ohne in schlechten Geschmack oder Kitsch abzugleiten. Gegnern der Pop-Art, Op-Art, des Hyperrealismus oder des Surrealismus, kurz, der Kunst des 20. Jahrhunderts, ist von einem Besuch bei Manolo abzuraten. Das gleiche gilt für jene, die vor der gewagten Zusammenstellung eines Rokokosofas mit einer Jugendstilstatuette, Kissen à la Versace und einem zeitgenössischen Gemälde in kräftigen Farben zurückschrecken. In Manolos »Höhle« wimmelt es von solchen Referenzen. Erwähnt sei, dass Julian Schnabel ganz und gar auf seinen Geschmack schwört, dass seine eigenen Bilder bald in einer New Yorker Galerie gezeigt werden und dass die Hotelgäste von dem charmanten Kunterbunt begeistert sind.

Song of the siren. The master of the house has wrought his art on this Barbie doll, transforming her into a fish-tailed mermaid perched atop a towel rail in the bathroom.

Die Barbiepuppe auf dem Handtuchhalter des Badezimmers hat der Hausherr in eine Sirene verwandelt.

Une Barbie transformée en sirène singulière signée par le maître de maison est posée sur le porte-serviettes de la salle de bains.

«Living about the shop», cette expression typiquement britannique illustre bien la situation de Manolo Rivero Cervera qui a installé son appartement au-dessus de son Hotel Trinidad et la Galerie Manolo Rivero réussit parfaitement à marier travail et vie privée. Rivero impressionne par sa passion pour l'art contemporain, son talent comme artiste et créateur et sa capacité à marier les objets, les meubles et les tableaux les plus divers sans tomber dans le mauvais goût et le kitsch. Evidemment rendre visite à Manolo n'est pas recommandé à ceux qui sont réfractaires au pop art, op art, hyperréalisme, surréalisme – en bref à l'art du 20e siècle, ni à ceux que la juxtaposition osée d'un canapé rocaille, d'une statuette Art nouveau, de quelques coussins à la Versace et d'un tableau contemporain aux vives couleurs fait frissonner d'horreur. La «caverne» de Manolo est remplie de références. Mentionnons que Julian Schnabel ne jure que par son goût, qu'une galerie de New York exposera bientôt ses propres œuvres et que les clients de son hôtel sont enchantés de ce merveilleux capharnaüm.

An Art Nouveau statue representing the moon stands in front of a picture window in the gallery.

Vor einer Glasfront der Galerie steht eine Jugendstilstatue, die den Mond symbolisiert.

Une statue 1900 symbolisant la lune se dresse devant l'une des baies vitrées de la galerie.

PREVIOUS PAGES: *The pool is only a few steps away from the gallery that leads to the salon filled with an impressive array of artwork and other treasures.*
LEFT: *Manolo has put together a bold personal collection in his residence. A giant canvas by José Bedia hangs alongside works by Jean-Paul Souchaud.*
FACING PAGE: *Manolo's works, exhibited in one of the rooms of the private gallery, bear witness to his own great talent as an artist.*

VORHERGEHENDE DOPPELSEITE: *Vom Swimmingpool sind es nur ein paar Schritte zur Galerie, die in den Salon führt, in dem sich zahlreiche Kunstwerke und Fundstücke aller Art befinden.*
LINKS: *In seiner Wohnung hat Manolo einfach alles zusammengetragen, was er liebt. Ein großes Gemälde von José Bedia wird von Werken von Jean-Paul Souchaud flankiert.*
RECHTE SEITE: *Manolos eigene Arbeiten, die in einem Raum seiner Galerie ausgestellt sind, belegen sein künstlerisches Talent.*

DOUBLE PAGE PRECEDENTE: *Quelques pas seulement séparent la piscine de la galerie qui mène au salon abritant de nombreuses œuvres d'art et des trouvailles en tout genre.*
A GAUCHE: *Dans sa demeure Manolo a assemblé avec audace ce qu'il aime. Un grand tableau de José Bedia est flanqué par des œuvres de Jean-Paul Souchaud.*
PAGE DE DROITE: *Les œuvres de Manolo exposées dans l'une des salles de sa galerie privée témoignent de son talent d'artiste.*

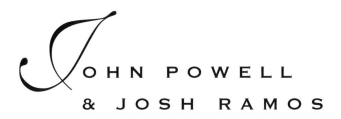

OHN POWELL
& JOSH RAMOS

Mérida

The Ermita de Santa Isabel is one of the oldest neighbourhoods in Mérida. And John Powell and Josh Ramos, who saved one of its four-centuries-old dwellings from destruction, can be thankful they began restoration work on the roof. Without that, they say, their home would never have withstood the ferocious storms that rage through the Yucatan on a regular basis. John Powell has enjoyed a multifarious career as an artistic director, painter, décor and costume designer, interior decorator, antiques dealer and fashion model. He has also worked as an assistant to John Saladino, Stephen Sills and Hervé Vanderstraeten. When Powell bought his home with partner Josh Ramos, a painter and fabric designer who works for many of the top fashion houses in Europe, Mexico and the U.S., the couple undertook eight exhausting months of restoration. Now, two years on, the oldest part of the quinta is filled with the couple's tasteful finds, resplendent with antique furniture, exquisite artwork and sacred objects. Thanks to their boundless energy and ideas, these two talented artists have breathed fascinating new life into an ancient abode.

Perched on top of a chest in the entrance hall, this colourful saint welcomes visitors on arrival.

Auf einer Truhe im Vestibül empfängt den Besucher eine farbenfrohe Heiligenfigur.

Posé sur un bahut du vestibule, un saint haut en couleurs accueille les visiteurs.

The shower room – the height of unadorned simplicity and understated chic!

Das Badezimmer – schnörkellos schlicht.

La salle d'eau – toute de sobriété et de dépouillement.

Ermita de Santa Isabel gehört zu den ältesten Stadtvierteln von Mérida und John Powell und Josh Ramos haben dort ein 400 Jahre altes Haus vor dem Ruin bewahrt. Sie sind froh, bei der Restaurierung mit dem Dach begonnen zu haben, andernfalls, so glauben sie, hätte der Bau einen jener verheerenden Stürme, die in regelmäßigen Abständen über Yucatán hinwegfegen, nicht überstanden. John war in seinem Leben wechselweise Artdirector, Maler, Bühnen- und Kostümbildner, Antiquar und Model. Außerdem hat er als Assistent von John Saladino, Stephen Sills und Hervé Vanderstraeten gearbeitet. Als John gemeinsam mit seinem Partner Josh Ramos, ebenfalls Maler und Stoffdesigner für namhafte Firmen in Europa, Mexiko und den USA, das Haus in Mérida erwarb, hatten die beiden mit enormen Problemen zu kämpfen und acht Monate aufreibende Restaurierungsarbeiten vor sich. Zwei Jahre nach dem ersten Spatenstich ist der älteste Trakt der Quinta mit passenden Fundstücken, schönen alten Möbeln, Kunstwerken und sakralen Kunstobjekten eingerichtet. Mit ihrem Ideenreichtum und ihrer Energie haben die beiden Künstler ihm ein faszinierendes Gesicht verliehen.

L'Ermita de Santa Isabel est l'un des plus vieux quartiers de Mérida, et John Powell et Josh Ramos qui y ont sauvé in extremis une maison de quatre siècles se félicitent d'avoir commencé par la restauration du toit. Selon eux, la demeure n'aurait pas résisté à une des tempêtes dévastatrices qui soufflent régulièrement sur le Yucatán. John a été tour à tour directeur artistique, peintre, créateur de décors et de costumes, décorateur, antiquaire et mannequin. Il a aussi été l'assistant de John Saladino, Stephen Sills et Hervé Vanderstraeten. En achetant cette maison à Mérida avec son partenaire Josh Ramos, lui-même peintre et qui crée des tissus pour des maisons renommées en Europe, au Mexique et aux Etats-Unis, John a dû affronter d'énormes problèmes et huit mois de restauration épuisante. Deux ans après le premier coup de pioche, la partie la plus ancienne de la quinta est remplie de trouvailles heureuses, de beaux meubles anciens, d'œuvres d'art et d'objets d'art sacré. Les deux artistes pleins d'idées et d'énergie lui ont donné un visage fascinant.

A detail of the stone, stucco and marble shower cubicle built by John Powell and Josh Ramos.

Die Duschkabine aus Stein, Stuck und Marmor, vom Hausherrn selbst gebaut.

Un détail de la cabine de douche en pierre, stuc et marbre construite par les maîtres de maison.

LEFT: *The rustic benches and Medici vase in the entrance hall give visitors a foretaste of the house's pure, simple décor.*

FACING PAGE: *John and Josh have made an interesting feature of the ruined walls around the courtyard: the pool and the water-lily filled ponds they built themselves.*

FOLLOWING PAGES: *The former designer and antique dealer have both marked the house with their sense of style.*

LINKS: *Im Eingangsbereich geben die rustikale Bank und eine Medici-Vase einen Vorgeschmack auf die schlichte Einrichtung.*

RECHTE SEITE: *In dem von ruinenhaften Mauern umgebenen Hof haben John und Josh ein Schwimmbecken und Seerosenteiche angelegt.*

FOLGENDE DOPPELSEITE: *Überall im Haus erkennt man die Handschrift des Ex-Designers und Antiquars.*

A GAUCHE: *Dans l'entrée, des bancs rustiques et un vase Médicis donnent un avant-goût de la sobriété du décor.*

PAGE DE DROITE: *John et Josh ont su tirer le meilleur parti des murs en ruines qui entourent la cour, la piscine et les bassins aux nénuphars construits par leurs soins.*

DOUBLE PAGE SUIVANTE: *Partout dans la maison, on reconnaît la griffe de l'ex-styliste et antiquaire.*

SALVADOR REYES RIOS & JOSEFINA LARRAIN LAGOS

Mérida

The streets of Yucatán's capital are a treasure trove of colonial architecture. Eyes never grow weary of contemplating late 19th-century wonders such as the Paseo de Montejo, lined with ornate stucco-decorated palaces and cut through with numbered alleyways filled with brightly coloured houses. The renowned Mexican architect Salvador Reyes Rios and his wife, designer Josefina Larrain Lagos, live here with their two children in a low-rise residence adorned with classical pilasters. Salvador and Josefina have restructured their turn-of-the-century home, giving it a resolutely contemporary feel, but their modern makeover integrates several historical features, such as cement flagstones and a beautiful colonnade leading onto the patio. The couple's pure tastes have also influenced the interiors. They have maintained a rustic spirit in the kitchen, a sober but comfortable style in the bathroom and decorated their home with stylishly minimalist furniture throughout. Their remarkable metamorphosis is completed with eye-catching details such as a striking section of blue wall, a strelitzia arranged in a vase and an elegant bathtub placed in the middle of the garden.

PREVIOUS PAGES: *The patio at the Reyes Rios residence extends into a leafy green garden which may not be vast, but where else would you find such a stylish outdoor bath?*
LEFT: *A strelitzia cuts a striking silhouette against the vivid blue background of the patio wall.*

VORHERGEHENDE DOPPELSEITE: *An den Hof des Hauses von Reyes Rios schließt sich ein kleiner Garten an. Dort steht eine Freiluftbadewanne aus Stein.*
LINKS: *Die schmale Silhouette einer Strelitzie hebt sich vom kräftigen Blau des Patios ab.*

DOUBLE PAGE PRECEDENTE: *Dans la maison des Reyes Rios, le patio est prolongé par un jardin de dimensions modestes mais qui abrite une baignoire en plein air!*
A GAUCHE: *La silhouette aiguë d'un strelitzia se découpe sur le mur bleu vif du patio.*

Wer in der Hauptstadt von Yucatán spazieren geht, kann die Schätze der Kolonialarchitektur des späten 19. Jahrhunderts bewundern. Man wird es einfach nicht satt, die Blicke über den Paseo de Montejo schweifen zu lassen. Viele mit Stuck verzierte Paläste stehen dort und ordentlich nummerierte Gassen, in denen sich Häuser in leuchtenden Farben reihen, kreuzen ihn. Salvador Reyes Rios, ein bekannter Architekt, und seine Frau Josefina Larrain Lagos, Designerin, bewohnen mit ihren beiden Kindern ein recht niedriges Haus, das mit klassischen Pfeilern geschmückt ist. Unter Erhaltung einiger Details dieser Epoche wie der Zementfliesen und des Säulengangs zum Patio haben die Besitzer die Räumlichkeiten jenseits der Toreinfahrt völlig neu gegliedert und diesem Haus aus der Jahrhundertwende ein entschieden modernes Ambiente verliehen. Auch das Interieur verrät den Wunsch nach Einfachheit. Das Paar hat die rustikale Küche behalten, ein komfortabel-funktionales Badezimmer eingerichtet und Möbel von mustergültiger Schlichtheit ausgesucht. Ein blauer Mauerabschnitt, eine Strelitzie in einer Vase und eine Badewanne im Garten vervollständigen diese bemerkenswerte Metamorphose.

The wicker lamp, designed by Josefina Larrain Lagos, echoes the lines of the patio columns.

Die von der Hausherrin entworfene Leuchte aus Korbweide harmoniert ausgezeichnet mit den Säulen im Hof.

Le luminaire en osier tressé conçu par la maîtresse de maison est en parfaite harmonie avec les colonnes du patio.

Se promener dans la capitale du Yucatán, c'est pouvoir admirer des trésors de l'architecture coloniale de la fin du 19ᵉ siècle. On ne se lasse pas de contempler le Paseo de Montejo bordé de palais décorés de «pâtisseries» en stuc et traversé de ruelles dûment numérotées où s'alignent des maisons aux couleurs vives. Salvador Reyes Rios, un architecte connu, et son épouse Josefina Larrain Lagos, designer, habitent avec leurs deux enfants une maison assez basse ornée de pilastres classiques. Au-delà de l'entrée cochère, les maîtres des lieux ont restructuré les espaces tout en gardant quelques détails d'époque comme les dalles de ciment et la colonnade qui donne accès au patio. Ils ont conféré à cette demeure fin de siècle une ambiance résolument contemporaine. L'intérieur montre le même souci de simplicité. Le couple a gardé la cuisine rustique, créé une salle de bains dépouillée et confortable et choisi des meubles d'une sobriété exemplaire. Un pan de mur bleu, un strelitzia dans un vase et une baignoire au milieu du jardin complètent cette métamorphose remarquable.

In the daytime, the hammock is rolled up into a ball and stored against the wall.

Tagsüber wird die aufgerollte Hängematte an der Wand eingehakt.

Le jour, le hamac roulé en boule est accroché au mur.

ABOVE: *A canopy is draped above the paved courtyard, providing shade from the sun.*
RIGHT: *The bed, inspired by the design of late 18th-century "pencil posts", was designed by the architect.*
FACING PAGE: *When siesta time approaches, roll down the hammock, snuggle up inside and dream your dreams in the deep blue depths of the patio.*

OBEN: *Ein Sonnensegel schützt den gepflasterten Hof vor der Mittagshitze.*
RECHTS: *Das Bett im »Pencil-Post«-Stil des ausgehenden 18. Jahrhunderts ist ein Entwurf des Architekten.*
RECHTE SEITE: *Während der Siesta kann man die Hängematte entrollen und im Blau des Patios träumen.*

CI-DESSUS: *Un vélum protège la cour pavée du grand soleil.*
A DROITE: *Le lit, inspiré des «pencil post» de la fin du 18ᵉ siècle, porte la signature de l'architecte.*
PAGE DE DROITE: *A l'heure de la sieste, on peut dérouler le hamac et rêver dans le bleu du patio.*

LEFT: *Interior shutters and wire meshing provide a cool retreat from the Mexican sun. In the narrow passageway near the dining room a slender cactus tapers towards the ceiling.*
FACING PAGE: *The owners have kept original design features in the kitchen, such as the traditional Mexican tilework and the impressive chimney hood.*

LINKS: *Die sich nach innen öffnenden Fensterläden sorgen für angenehme Kühle. Im schmalen Durchgang am Esszimmer ragt schlank ein Kaktus auf.*
RECHTE SEITE: *In der Küche sind die traditionelle mexikanische Kachelung und der großzügig bemessene Rauchfang erhalten geblieben.*

A GAUCHE: *Les volets intérieurs et les grillages dispensent une fraîcheur agréable. Un étroit passage près de la salle à manger abrite un cactus élancé.*
PAGE DE DROITE: *La cuisine a conservé son carrelage traditionnel mexicain et sa hotte aux dimensions généreuses.*

The furniture Salvador Reyes Rios designed for the living room reflects this architect's love of pure, clean lines. The overhead skylight built into the ceiling makes clever use of natural light.

Im Wohnzimmer kündet das vom Architekten selbst entworfene Mobiliar von seiner Vorliebe für klare Formen. Das Licht fällt durch einen geschickt in die Decke eingelassenen Dachreiter ein.

Dans le séjour, le mobilier dessiné par l'architecte reflète sa prédilection pour les lignes pures. La lumière zénithale provient d'un lanterneau habilement intégré au plafond.

$\mathscr{A}$ PALAPA HOUSE

Josefina Espejo

Mérida

Coming upon Colonia La Ceiba, visitors will be pleasantly surprised by the characteristic charms of this residential neighbourhood in Mérida and impressed by the wide variety of forms, architectural styles and eye-catching colours. From a Le Corbusier-style villa and a residence influenced by the palette and minimalism of Luis Barragán to a sturdy house where natural materials and neutral tones dominate, a host of different architects have let their creative imagination run riot. And you can understand why Josefina Espejo and her architects Luis Torres Perazza and Alvaro Ponce Espejo chose to experiment with something a little out of the ordinary, too. Josefina, whose main aim was to create a cool and light-filled family home, "open to the four winds," adopted the form of the traditional palapa. The result is a spacious, open-sided dwelling with a thatched roof that looks out onto terraces, a Californian-style pool and a second palapa, housing a restaurant and a children's play area. A truly original way of living and communing with nature!

PREVIOUS PAGES: *Minimalist contemporary architecture merges with the traditional form of the palapa.*
LEFT: *A cactus stands on a console behind the palapa.*

VORHERGEHENDE DOPPELSEITE: *Die sachlichen Umrisse zeitgenössischer Architektur gehen eine raffinierte Verbindung mit der traditionellen Palapa ein.*
LINKS: *Auf einer Konsole hinter der Palapa steht ein Kaktus.*

DOUBLE PAGE PRECEDENTE: *Les lignes sobres de l'architecture contemporaine sont astucieusement mariées à celles de la palapa traditionnelle.*
A GAUCHE: *Un cactus s'épanouit sur une console derrière la palapa.*

Nähert man sich der Colonia La Ceiba, einem Residenzviertel am Rande von Mérida, so ist man angenehm überrascht von der ausgesprochen charaktervollen Erscheinung des Bauensembles. Eine Vielzahl von Stilen, einladenden Formen und Farben beherrschen das Bild – von der Villa im Stil Le Corbusiers über ein Wohnhaus, das sich an die Strenge und Farbgebung Luis Barragáns hält, bis zum robusten Landhaus mit natürlichen Baustoffen und neutralen Tönen. Der Erfindungsgeist der verschiedenen Architekten ist beeindruckend und man versteht sofort, weshalb Josefina Espejo und ihre Architekten Luis Torres Perazza und Alvaro Ponce Espejo ebenfalls beschlossen haben, neue Wege zu gehen. Mit dem Ziel, ein helles, kühles und nach allen Seiten offenes Einfamilienhaus zu bauen, hat Josefina die Form einer traditionellen Palapa gewählt. Heute öffnet dieses große, mit Stroh gedeckte Sonnendach auf verschiedene Terrassen, einen Swimmingpool im kalifornischen Stil und eine weitere Palapa, in der sich ein Restaurant und Spielflächen für die Kinder befinden. Eine originelle und angenehme Art, im Freien zu leben.

Built in pure Mexican style, the car port belies its true nature. Only close observation reveals its true function as a garage.

Jedes Detail des im reinsten mexikanischen Stil gebauten Carports verleugnet seine eigentliche Funktion.

Chaque détail du «car port» construit dans le plus pur style mexicain démentit sa vraie fonction.

En s'approchant de la Colonia La Ceiba, un quartier résidentiel aux confins de Mérida, le visiteur est agréablement surpris par l'aspect très caractéristique de l'ensemble et par une grande variété de styles, de formes et de couleurs attrayantes. De la ville style Le Corbusier à la demeure influencée par la rigueur et la palette de Barragán, en passant par la robuste maison où dominent les matériaux naturels et les teintes neutres, on est séduit par l'esprit inventif des différents architectes. Et l'on comprend pourquoi Josefina Espejo et ses architectes Luis Torres Perazza et Alvaro Ponce Espejo ont choisi à leur tour de quitter les sentiers battus. Soucieux de créer une maison de famille lumineuse, fraîche et «ouverte à tous les vents», Josefina a adopté la forme de la palapa traditionnelle. Aujourd'hui ce grand parasol coiffé de chaume s'ouvre sur des terrasses, une piscine californienne et une autre palapa qui abrite un restaurant et des aires de jeux pour les enfants. Une façon originale et agréable de vivre en plein air.

Framed against the red ochre walls of a small courtyard, a sapling spreads its branches in the sun.

In dem kleinen rot-ocker getünchten Hof streckt ein junger Baum seine Äste der Sonne entgegen.

Dans une petite cour aux murs badigeonnés d'ocre rouge, un jeune arbre tend ses branches vers le soleil.

LEFT: *An artistically positioned tree trunk by the pool serves as a piece of contemporary sculpture.*
FACING PAGE: *Hidden amongst a sway of banana trees and towering palms, this paradisiacal palapa makes the perfect outdoor living and dining room.*

LINKS: *Der Baumstamm neben dem Swimmingpool wirkt wie eine moderne Skulptur.*
RECHTE SEITE: *Von Bananenstauden und Palmen umgeben, dient diese wunderschöne Palapa als Wohn- und Esszimmer im Freien.*

A GAUCHE: *Près de la piscine, un tronc d'arbre fait office de sculpture contemporaine.*
PAGE DE DROITE: *La magnifique palapa entourée de bananiers et de palmiers sert de séjour et de salle à manger en plein air.*

FACING PAGE: *Children love to play in this second, smaller palapa built at the bottom of the garden.*
RIGHT: *Gnarled tree trunks form a natural colonnade, separating the entrance from the inner courtyard and the car port.*

LINKE SEITE: *Eine zweite, bescheidenere Palapa wurde im hinteren Teil des Gartens errichtet. Die Kinder spielen dort besonders gern.*
RECHTS: *Mächtige Baumstämme bilden eine Art Kolonnade, die den Eingangsbereich von Innenhof und Carport trennt.*

PAGE DE GAUCHE: *Une seconde palapa, plus modeste, a été édifiée au fond du jardin. Les enfants adorent y jouer.*
A DROITE: *De gros troncs d'arbre forment la colonnade qui sépare l'entrée de la cour intérieure et de l'abri à voitures.*

$\mathcal{H}$ACIENDA XCUMPICH

Sylviane Boucher Le Landais

Mérida

The Xcumpich, a magnificent hacienda dating back to the latter half of the 19th century, lies just north of Mérida. The hacienda's "casa principal" is secluded behind a high stone wall, which protects the house's blood-red façade, imposing portico and neoclassical columns from passing eyes. When Sylviane Boucher Le Landais, the famous French archaeologist and Mayan ceramics specialist, bought the Xcumpich in 1984, this historically important house was a pile of ruins. Following Sylviane through this splendid residence today, it is hard to imagine the sheer extent of rebuilding and restructuring work it required. The main living room (the former "sala") on the garden side of the house has been embellished with a gallery of thick columns. And its immaculate whiteness makes a dramatic contrast with the deep red of the entrance and the warm golden yellow of the dining room. Traditional furniture and folkloric objects are played off against the house's simple architecture elsewhere. In the lush green garden a fountain adorned with smiling cherubs plays, its tranquil splashing the only sound in this oasis of quiet beauty.

PREVIOUS PAGES: *Hacienda Xcumpich boasts an eye-catching façade, embellished with arches and classical columns.*
LEFT: *Framed against a striking red wall, this Mexican mask fixes passers-by with its beady bird's eyes.*

VORHERGEHENDE DOPPELSEITE: *Die Hacienda Xcumpich besitzt eine prächtige, mit klassischen Bögen und Säulen geschmückte Fassade.*
LINKS: *Von einer kräftig roten Mauer fixiert eine mexikanische Maske den Besucher mit runden Vogelaugen.*

DOUBLE PAGE PRECEDENTE: *L'Hacienda Xcumpich possède une magnifique façade ornée d'arches et de colonnes classiques.*
A GAUCHE: *Sur le mur rouge vif, un masque mexicain nous fixe de ses yeux ronds d'oiseau.*

Die »casa principal« der Hacienda Xcumpich, die im Norden von Mérida liegt und aus der zweiten Hälfte des 19. Jahrhunderts stammt, ist von einer hohen Mauer umgeben, hinter der sich eine blutrote Fassade, großzügige Proportionen, ein imposanter Portikus und klassizistische Säulen verbergen. Als die gebürtige Französin Sylviane Boucher Le Landais, eine angesehene Archäologin und Spezialistin für Mayakeramiken, 1984 die Hacienda kaufte, standen von dem einst so wunderbaren Gebäude nur noch Ruinen. Wer heute als Besucher mit Sylviane durch die Räume geht, kann sich den Umfang der geleisteten Arbeiten kaum vorstellen. Das große Wohnzimmer, die frühere »sala«, liegt zum Garten und wird heute durch eine Galerie mit stabilen Säulen verschönert. Die makellosen Weißtöne kontrastieren mit dem tiefen Rot des Eingangsbereichs und dem Goldgelb des Esszimmers. Traditionelle Möbel und volkskunstliche Objekte ergänzen die schnörkellose Architektur perfekt. Im Garten plätschert ein mit pausbäckigen Cherubinen verzierter Springbrunnen, der Xcumpich zu einer Oase der Schönheit werden lässt.

La «casa principal» de l'Hacienda Xcumpich, située au nord de Mérida et qui date de la seconde moitie du 19ᵉ siècle, est entourée d'un haut mur qui dissimule sa façade couleur sang de bœuf et ses proportions généreuses, son portique imposant et ses colonnes néoclassiques. Lorsque Sylviane Boucher Le Landais, Française de naissance, archéologue renommée et spécialiste des céramiques mayas, l'a acquise en 1984, il ne restait plus que ruines de cette maison au passé prestigieux. En suivant aujourd'hui Sylviane à travers la demeure, le visiteur peut difficilement s'imaginer l'ampleur des travaux accomplis. Le grand salon (l'ancienne «sala») côté jardin a été embelli par une galerie aux robustes colonnes. Sa blancheur immaculée contraste avec le rouge soutenu de l'entrée et le jaune doré de la salle à manger; les meubles traditionnels et des objets populaires se marient parfaitement à l'architecture dépouillée. Dans le jardin, une fontaine couronnée de chérubins joufflus murmure sur un fond de verdure luxuriant, faisant de Xcumpich une oasis de beauté.

The sunflower yellow walls of the dining room provide a vivid burst of colour.

Das Esszimmer ist in Sonnenblumengelb gehalten.

La salle à manger avec ses murs jaune tournesol.

FACING PAGE: *Like all haciendas built at the time of the "green gold" rush, Xcumpich is a marvel of colonial architecture.*
ABOVE: *The rustically appointed dining room beckons lovers of Mexican cuisine, which is as tasty as it is spicy.*
RIGHT: *an enamel-coated iron wash-basin surrounded by various decorative objects.*

LINKE SEITE: *Wie alle in der Zeit des »grünen Goldes« erbauten Haciendas, beeindruckt auch Xcumpich mit nobler Kolonial-architektur.*
OBEN: *Im Esszimmer erwartet den Liebhaber der ebenso schmackhaften wie scharfen mexikanischen Küche eine rustikale Einrichtung.*
RECHTS: *Das emaillierte Eisenbecken ist von verschiedenen Dekorationsstücken um-geben.*

PAGE DE GAUCHE: *Comme toutes les haciendas construites à l'époque de l'«or vert», Xcumpich présente une architecture coloniale impressionnante et riche.*
CI-DESSUS: *Dans la salle à manger un robuste mobilier campagnard accueille les amateurs d'une cuisine mexicaine savoureuse et épicée.*
A DROITE: *un lave-mains en fonte émaillée entouré de divers objets décoratifs.*

$\mathcal{H}$ACIENDA PETAC

Dev & Chuck Stern

Yucatan

The Mayans made their mark on the Yucatan peninsula over more than four thousand years. And today the pyramids of Uxmal, Chichén Itzá and Tulum stand as a testimony to their unique culture, which fell into decline after the arrival of the conquistadors, and almost disappeared from the face of the earth altogether. The Mayans, a fiercely proud race, were reduced to slavery and set to work building the main colonial towns. They were also employed at the haciendas working sisal, a fibre from the henequen (a native Mexican plant). In the early 20th century, synthetic fibres replaced this "green gold" and, like the Mayan temples, the haciendas crumbled into oblivion, most of them standing as ruins today. Fortunately, Texan couple Dev and Chuck Stern stepped in to save Hacienda Petac, a splendid residence located in Petac, a pleasant drive from the town of Mérida. With the help of architect Salvador Reyes Rios, the Sterns restored Hacienda Petac to its former glory. Today the hacienda is run as a luxury guesthouse, its intimate atmosphere, home comforts and cuisine and its Moorish beauty leaving a lasting impression on all who stay here.

PREVIOUS PAGES: *The hammocks hung by the hacienda pool beckon with promises of siestas and sweet afternoon dreams.*
LEFT: *Former opera singer Gabriel plies his artistic talent in the kitchen these days, cooking up traditional Mexican dishes and regional specialities.*

VORHERGEHENDE DOPPELSEITE: *Die am Swimmingpool der Hacienda angebrachten Hängematten laden zum Ausruhen ein.*
LINKS: *Gabriel, Ex-Opernsänger und talentierter Koch, bereitet köstliche mexikanische Spezialitäten zu.*

DOUBLE PAGE PRECEDENTE: *Les hamacs suspendus près de la piscine de l'hacienda invitent au doux repos.*
A GAUCHE: *Gabriel, ex-chanteur d'opéra et cuisinier talentueux, prépare des spécialités mexicaines qui font sa fierté.*

Über 4000 Jahre lang haben die Mayas die Halbinsel Yucatán geprägt. Noch heute zeugen die Pyramiden von Uxmal, Chichén Itzá und Tulum von einer unerreichten Kultur, die nach dem Eintreffen der Conquistadores ihren Niedergang erlebte und beinahe für immer verschwunden wäre. Als Sklaven wirkten die stolzen Mayas am Bau der Kolonialstädte mit und verarbeiteten auf den großen Haciendas Sisal, eine Faser, die vom so genannten Hennequen (der Silberagave) stammt. Zu Beginn des 20. Jahrhunderts lösten Synthetikfasern das »grüne Gold« ab, wodurch die Haciendas, wie schon zuvor die Mayatempel, dem Untergang geweiht wurden und heute oftmals in Trümmern liegen. Diese beeindruckende Hacienda, die von der Stadt Mérida bequem zu erreichen ist, wurde im letzten Augenblick von dem texanischen Paar Dev und Chuck Stern gerettet. Der Architekt Salvador Reyes Rios verhalf ihr wieder zu ihrem einstigen Glanz. Heute stellen Bewirtung, Komfort, Gastronomie und die von maurischen Stilelementen geprägte Schönheit des Bauwerks auch anspruchsvollste Gäste zufrieden.

A flame-coloured strelitzia blazes against a red-ochre wall, deploying the full range of Mexico's sumptuous palette.

Eine feuerrote Strelitzie vor rot-ockerfarbenem Hintergrund. Die mexikanische Farbenpalette ist denkbar schillernd.

Un strelitzia couleur feu sur un fond ocre rouge. La palette mexicaine est chatoyante à souhait.

Pendant plus de quatre mille ans, les Mayas ont marqué de leur présence la péninsule du Yucatán. De nos jours, les pyramides d'Uxmal, Chichén Itzá et Tulum témoignent d'une culture inégalée qui connut son déclin après l'arrivée des conquistadores et qui faillit ensuite disparaître à tout jamais. Devenus esclaves, les fiers Mayas ont participé à la construction des grandes villes coloniales et ont travaillé le sisal, une fibre issue du «hennequen» (une variété d'agave) dans les grandes haciendas. Au début du 20e siècle, la fibre synthétique a supplanté «l'or vert» et, à l'instar des temples mayas, les haciendas ont été condamnées au déclin et souvent ne sont plus que ruines. Sauvée in extremis par Dev et Chuck Stern, un couple texan, la magnifique Hacienda Petac à Petac, située à une distance agréable de la ville de Mérida, a retrouvé sa splendeur d'antan avec l'aide de l'architecte Salvador Reyes Rios. Aujourd'hui, l'accueil, le confort, la gastronomie et la beauté mauresque des lieux satisfont les hôtes les plus exigeants et leur laissent un souvenir inoubliable.

A Mexican nosegay adds a spray of colour to a bathroom alcove.

Der kleine Blumenstrauß in der Wandnische bringt zusätzlich Farbe ins Badezimmer.

Dans une des salles de bains, un petit bouquet charmant dans une niche.

ABOVE: *Centuries on, the hacienda's old stone reservoir has been converted into a swimming pool.*
RIGHT: *Water spews down into this antique trough in the grand old tradition of Italian Renaissance villas.*

OBEN: *Die alte Wasserzisterne wird heute als Schwimmbecken sehr geschätzt.*
RECHTS: *In der Tradition italienischer Renaissancevillen speisen zahlreiche Wasserspeier die alte Tränke.*

CI-DESSUS: *L'ancien réservoir d'eau est devenu une piscine très appréciée.*
A DROITE: *Dans la grande tradition des villas italiennes de la Renaissance, un ancien abreuvoir est alimenté en eau par de nombreux cracheurs.*

ABOVE: *Traces of An-dalusian architecture are evident in the patio's stunning Moorish arches.*
RIGHT: *A garden path winds across the im-maculately kept lawn, leading to the terrace, the antique trough and the "master's house", where the plantation owner once lived.*

OBEN: *Der mit mau-rischem Bogenwerk versehene Patio verrät den Einfluss der anda-lusischen Architektur.*
RECHTS: *Über den gepflegten Rasen führt ein Weg zur Terrasse, der alten Tränke und dem Haus des Eigentü-mers, in dem einst der Großgrundbesitzer wohnte.*

CI-DESSUS: *Le patio agrémenté d'arches mauresques trahit l'in-fluence de l'architecture andalouse.*
A DROITE: *Un chemin tracé dans le gazon très soigné mène à l'abreu-voir, à la terrasse et à la maison du patron, où logeait jadis le proprié-taire.*

The architect has made a feature of the passageway leading to the old machine room, adding an ornamental fountain and symmetrical rows of palm trees.

Den Durchgang zur ehemaligen Maschinenhalle hat der Architekt mit einem Zierspringbrunnen und symmetrisch angeordneten Palmen verschönert.

L'architecte a enrichi l'ancien passage menant à la salle des machines d'une fontaine-bassin ornementale et de palmiers plantés de manière symétrique.

PREVIOUS PAGES: *The hacienda has been magnificently restored. Visitors can escape the blaze of the midday sun in one of the cool, shady patios in the entrance hall. The stone hangar enjoys a second lease of life as a billiard and games room.*
RIGHT: *The hammocks hanging in the the dining room bear witness to the fact that in the olden days any room in the house could function as a dormitory at any hour of the day.*

VORHERGEHENDE DOPPELSEITE: *Die Hacienda ist meisterhaft restauriert. In einem der Patios im Eingangsbereich können die Besucher sich in der Kühle und im gedämpften Licht entspannen, oder sie verbringen einen Abend im Hangar, der zu einem Billard- und Spielsaal umgewandelt wurde.*
RECHTS: *Die Hängematten im Esszimmer weisen darauf hin, dass einst jeder Raum zu jeder Tageszeit in ein Schlafzimmer umfunktioniert werden konnte.*

DOUBLE PAGE PRECEDENTE: *L'hacienda a été magistralement restaurée. Dans l'un des patios de l'entrée, les visiteurs peuvent se détendre dans la fraîcheur et la lumière tamisée, et passer une soirée dans le hangar qui a été transformé en salle de billard et de jeux.*
A DROITE: *Dans la salle à manger la présence des hamacs prouve qu'autrefois chaque pièce pouvait être transformée en dortoir à tout moment de la journée.*

LEFT: *In the bath-rooms natural materials were favoured.*
FACING PAGE: *A bedroom is decorated with traditional dia-mond tiling and twin four-poster beds draped in mosquito nets.*
PAGES 108–109: *The mirror and the exquisite restoration work on the ancient chapel are a testimony to the beauty of Mex-ican handicraft.*
PAGES 110–111: *Mayan girls dressed in traditional embroidered "huipiles".*

LINKS: *Im Badezim-mer wurden natürliche Materialien bevorzugt.*
RECHTE SEITE: *Eines der Zimmer hat rauten-förmige Bodenfliesen, dazu zwei identische Betten mit Moskito-netzen.*
SEITE 108–109: *Der Spiegel und die muster-gültige Restaurierung der alten Kapelle zeugen von der Qualität mexi-kanischen Kunsthand-werks.*
SEITE 110–111: *Maya-Mädchen in tra-ditionellen bestickten »huipiles«.*

A GAUCHE: *Dans les salles de bains dominent les matériaux naturels.*
PAGE DE DROITE: *Une des chambres est agrémentée d'un dallage en losanges, de lits jumeaux à colonnes coiffés de moustiquaires.*
PAGES 108–109: *Le miroir et la restauration exemplaire de l'ancien-ne chapelle témoignent de la qualité indéniable de l'artisanat mexicain.*
PAGES 110–111: *Des jeunes filles mayas parées de leurs huipiles brodés traditionnels.*

HACIENDA POXILA

Alejandro Patrón Laviada

Mérida

The Hacienda Poxila stands on the Camino Real, a road link-ing Mérida to Campeche, a fortress on the west coast of Yuca-tan that was pillaged and destroyed by French, English and Dutch pirates. Like most of the other important estancias in the region, the Poxila partly dates back to the 16th century. The hacienda thrived under its owner, maize producer Lorenzo Mateo Caldera, in the 18th century, but enjoyed a veritable golden age in the next thanks to the cultivation of sisal. Under the management of the Lara family, the Poxila went on to be-come the impressive neoclassical residence it is today. Like all haciendas in Yucatan, the Poxila is made up of a sumptuous master's house, a machine room and a number of smaller out-buildings that constitute the workers' quarters. The Poxila's current owner, Alejandro Patrón Laviada, runs the place in masterly fashion and looks back on "the good old days" with a certain nostalgia. The Poxila's interiors abound with religious objects and antique furniture, while outside the lush green gardens are filled with the sound of fountains and birdsong.

PREVIOUS PAGES: *Thanks to the passion and unswerving deter-mination of its owner the Hacienda Poxila has maintained its imposing colonial architecture.*
LEFT: *A fragment of a 19th-century painted wooden Pietà. The Vir-gin's face is shrouded in a black lace veil.*

VORHERGEHENDE DOPPELSEITE: *Mit Enthusiasmus und Ein-satz rettete der neue Eigentümer die ebenso sachliche wie eindrucks-volle Architektur der Hacienda.*
LINKS: *Detail einer farbigen Holz-Pietà aus dem 19. Jahrhundert. Die Jungfrau trägt einen schwarzen Spit-zenschleier.*

DOUBLE PAGE PRE-CEDENTE: *L'architec-ture sobre et impression-nante de l'Hacienda Poxila a été sauvée par l'enthousiasme et les ef-forts de son propriétaire.*
A GAUCHE: *Un frag-ment d'une pietà en bois polychromé 19ᵉ. La Vierge porte un voile de dentelle noire.*

Die Hacienda Poxila liegt am Camino Real, der Mérida mit Campeche verbindet, einer Festungsstadt an der Westküste von Yucatán, die von französischen, englischen und holländischen Piraten mehrfach geplündert und geschliffen worden ist. Wie die meisten bedeutenden Estancias stammt die Anlage aus dem 16. Jahrhundert. Im 18. Jahrhundert brachte es ihr Eigentümer Lorenzo Mateo Caldera mit dem Maisanbau zu Wohlstand, ihre Blütezeit erlebte sie jedoch im 19. Jahrhundert durch die Sisalproduktion. Unter der Obhut der Familie Lara nahm Poxila die beeindruckende klassizistische Gestalt von heute an. Wie alle Haciendas in Yucatán besteht Poxila aus einem prächtigen Herrenhaus, einer Maschinenhalle und mehreren Nebengebäuden für das Personal. Der heutige Besitzer, Alejandro Patrón Laviada, leitet die Hacienda mit gelassener Autorität und beschwört gerne die »gute alte Zeit« herauf. Heute stehen in den Innenräumen wieder alte Möbel und schöne Sakralobjekte und im Garten vermischt sich das Plätschern der Springbrunnen mit dem Gezwitscher der Vögel.

A 19th-century wooden cross leans against a wall daubed in yellow ochre.

Nahe dem Eingang ein Holzkreuz aus dem 19. Jahrhundert vor einer ockergelb getünchten Mauer.

Près de l'entrée, une croix en bois 19ᵉ devant un mur badigeonné d'ocre jaune.

L'Hacienda Poxila se trouve sur le Camino Real qui relie Mérida à Campeche, une forteresse située sur la côte ouest du Yucatán et qui fut pillée et détruite plusieurs fois par des pirates français, anglais et hollandais. Elle date en partie du 16ᵉ siècle, comme la plupart des plus importantes estancias. Au 18ᵉ siècle, elle s'est enrichie sous son propriétaire Lorenzo Mateo Caldera, producteur de maïs, mais c'est au 19ᵉ siècle qu'elle a connu son âge d'or avec le sisal. Gérée par la famille Lara, Poxila est devenue le bâtiment impressionnant d'aspect néoclassique que l'on connaît aujourd'hui. Comme toutes les haciendas du Yucatán, Poxila est composée d'une somptueuse maison de maître, d'une salle des machines et de plusieurs dépendances pour le personnel. L'actuel propriétaire, Alejandro Patrón Laviada, dirige l'hacienda de main de maître et sait évoquer le «bon vieux temps». Aujourd'hui, les intérieurs abritent à nouveau des meubles anciens et de beaux objets religieux, et, dans les jardins verdoyants, le murmure des fontaines se marie aux cris des oiseaux.

Lush green foliage makes a colourful contrast against this flame-red wall.

Die feuerrote Mauer und die üppig wuchernden Pflanzen ergänzen sich auf ganz natürliche Weise.

Le mur couleur feu et les plantes luxuriantes s'épousent tout naturellement.

PREVIOUS PAGES: *Objects of strange and unsettling beauty. A battered wooden wheel leans against an ancient wall with paint flaking off like parchment. The brick-coloured stucco façades of the workers' former living quarters and the machine room were left unaltered.*
RIGHT: *The 19th-century furniture in the master bedroom, where vast spaces echo like a ballroom, hark back to a golden age of charm and prosperity. A Virgin and child cast protective glances over the bed*

VORHERGEHENDE DOPPELSEITE: *Ein wurmstichiges Holzrad vor einer blättrigen Mauer – ein ungewöhnliches Schmuckmotiv. Die frühere Dienstbotenwohnung und die Maschinenhalle haben ihre mit ziegelrotem Gips verputzten Fassaden behalten.*
RECHTS: *Im Hauptschlafzimmer, weitläufig wie ein Ballsaal, erinnert das Mobiliar aus dem 19. Jahrhundert an eine glanzvolle Zeit. Eine Madonna mit Kind hängt über dem Kopfende des Bettes.*

DOUBLE PAGE PRECEDENTE: *Une roue en bois vermoulu, contre un mur à la peinture écaillée – un objet décoratif insolite. L'ancien logis du personnel et la salle aux machines ont gardé leurs façades enduites de stuc couleur brique.*
A DROITE: *Dans la chambre maîtresse, vaste comme une salle de bal, le mobilier 19e évoque une époque prospère et pleine de charme. Une Vierge à l'enfant domine la tête de lit.*

LEFT: *A heart-shaped candle-holder in the private chapel is still bedecked with religious candles and votive offerings.*
FACING PAGE: *In bygone days Mexican interiors were filled with religious paintings and saintly icons. Alejandro Patrón Laviada has recreated this holy atmosphere in his 21st-century home.*

LINKS: *Nach wie vor ist die Privatkapelle ein Raum der Andacht mit Kerzen in dem herzförmigen Kandelaber.*
RECHTE SEITE: *Früher fanden sich in den mexikanischen Innenräumen zahlreiche Heiligenbilder und -statuen. Alejandro Patrón Laviada hat es verstanden, diese von aufrichtigem Glaubensgefühl geprägte Atmosphäre wieder herzustellen.*

A GAUCHE: *Dans la chapelle privée, le porte-cierges en forme de cœur accueille toujours les bougies et les vœux d'espoir.*
PAGE DE DROITE: *Autrefois, les intérieurs mexicains abritaient de nombreux tableaux et statues de saints. Alejandro Patrón Laviada a su reconstituer cette ambiance imprégnée d'un sentiment religieux sincère.*

 TRADITIONAL MAYAN HOUSE

Hacienda Yaxcopoil

Yucatan

Traditional Mayan houses are a frequent sight when travelling through Yucatan. Dotted along country roads beside their more imposing neighbours, the haciendas, many of these houses are centuries old. Built out of stone debris covered in plaster, with their original thatched roofs often replaced by corrugated iron, these modest dwellings offer as little comfort as in bygone days. And yet extreme poverty and harsh living conditions have not destroyed their beauty. The families who live here on simple mud floors possess nothing more than a hammock, a few pieces of furniture and a handful of kitchen utensils. Rooms are lit by neon light and house a fridge and a simple home altar decorated with religious icons, candles and a tiny pile of personal mementoes for prayer and communication with their dead. These ancestors worked for a pittance at the local haciendas, their children and pet dogs their only assets in life. These Mayan houses will doubtless be standing for many more years to come, housing future generations of rural workers.

The mistress of the house sits in the doorway, taking a break from her chores.

Vor der Tür ihrer Wohnung genießt die Hausherrin eine Atempause.

La maîtresse de maison profite d'un moment de détente devant la porte de son logis.

Wenn man Yucatán bereist, gewöhnt man sich rasch an die Mayahäuser, die man an den Feldwegen nahe der imposanten Haciendas zu sehen bekommt. Die mitunter jahrhundertealten Gebäude, errichtet aus mit Gips verputzten Steinbrocken und vielfach mit Wellblech und nicht mehr mit Stroh gedeckt, sind heute wie damals wenig komfortabel. Sie bieten Familien Unterkunft, die sich trotz äußerster Armut und schwierigen Lebensbedingungen den Sinn für das Schöne bewahrt haben. Der Boden unter den Füßen der Bewohner besteht aus fest gestampfter Erde und sie begnügen sich mit ein paar Möbelstücken, einer Hängematte und dem einen oder anderen Kochutensil. Viel Wert hingegen legen sie darauf, dass es Neonlicht gibt, einen Kühlschrank und einen Hausaltar. Hier stehen Andachtsbilder, Kerzen und eine Vielzahl persönlicher Erinnerungsstücke, um zu beten und mit den Verstorbenen, die ihnen am Herzen liegen, in Verbindung zu bleiben. Schon ihre Vorfahren haben gegen mageren Lohn auf den Haciendas gearbeitet, Kinder und Hunde waren ihr ganzer Reichtum. Und wahrscheinlich werden die Mayahäuser auf dieselbe Weise auch künftige Generationen beherbergen.

En parcourant le Yucatán, on s'habitue vite à contempler les maisons mayas disposées le long des chemins de campagne à proximité des imposantes haciendas. Parfois âgées de plusieurs siècles et édifiées avec des débris de pierres recouverts de plâtre, le chaume du toit souvent remplacé par la tôle ondulée, aussi peu confortables qu'autrefois, elles offrent un refuge à des familles dont l'extrême pauvreté et les conditions de vie difficiles n'affectent pas le sens du beau. Leurs habitants qui foulent un sol en terre battue, se contentent de quelques meubles, d'un hamac et de quelques ustensiles de cuisine, insistent sur la présence d'un éclairage au néon, d'un réfrigérateur et d'un autel domestique où les images pieuses, quelques bougies et un amoncellement de souvenirs sentimentaux leur permettent de prier et de communiquer avec leurs chers disparus. Leurs ancêtres ont travaillé pour un maigre salaire dans les haciendas, n'ayant pour toute richesse que leurs enfants et leurs chiens. Les maisons mayas continueront sans doute à abriter ainsi les générations à venir.

ABOVE: *These traditional Mayan houses are a frequent sight when travelling through Yucatan. The simple stone abodes house rural workers and their families.*

RIGHT AND FACING PAGE: *All Mayan houses are equipped with the traditional hammock and a home altar dedicated to the saints and the "Holy Virgin of Guadalupe".*

OBEN: *In Yucatán gibt es zahlreiche traditionelle Häuser. Nach wie vor leben darin die ärmsten Familien.*

RECHTS UND RECHTE SEITE: *Kein Mayahaus ohne Hängematte und ohne einen kleinen Altar, der den Heiligen und der Jungfrau von Guadalupe geweiht ist.*

CI-DESSUS: *Les maisons traditionnelles sont nombreuses au Yucatán. Elles continuent d'héberger les familles les plus modestes.*

A DROITE ET PAGE DE DROITE: *Pas de maison maya sans hamac et sans petit autel consacré aux saints et à la Vierge de Guadalupe.*

A CONVERTED MAYAN HOUSE

Hacienda San José

Cacalchen

A tragic destiny befell Yucatan's haciendas when production of the "green gold" (sisal) practically died out in the region. Occasionally the vestiges of what were once veritable palaces can be glimpsed through the Moorish arches of an antique portal. But many of these magnificent dwellings have long since crumbled into ruin. Not so the Hacienda San José, which stands as proudly as ever on the road between Mérida and Tekantó. Recently restored to its past glory by Starwood Hotels & Resorts, the hacienda is now the height of 21st-century comfort and sophistication. Guests, who are attracted by San José's history and its breathtaking location, also appreciate the atmosphere of calm and well-being that reigns here. Those seeking an original place to stay, secluded from prying eyes, will adore the old Mayan house, which stands, according to hacienda tradition, in the shadow of the "casa del duegno". The house has been superbly restored by the architect Salvador Reyes Rios, who has managed to transform the former plantation workers' quarters into a luxurious modern guesthouse.

The gnarled roots of an ancient tree in the park snake across the grass like tentacles.

Wie Tentakel sehen die gewundenen Wurzeln eines Baumes im Park aus.

Dans le parc, les racines tortueuses d'un arbre ressemblent à des tentacules.

Die Haciendas in Yucatán ereilte ein trauriges Schicksal, als die Produktion des »grünen Goldes«, des Sisals, praktisch eingestellt wurde. Viele dieser großartigen Bauwerke liegen in Trümmern. Hier und da erblickt der Besucher hinter einem Portal mit maurischem Bogenwerk die verwitterten Überreste ehemals palastartiger Bauten. Umso erstaunter und erfreuter ist man beim Anblick der Hacienda San José, die an der Straße zwischen Mérida und Tekantó liegt und in ihrer einstigen Schönheit wieder errichtet wurde. Nach der Restaurierung durch Starwood Hotels & Resorts sieht das Gebäude, mit raffiniertestem Komfort ausgestattet, dem 21. Jahrhundert entgehen. Die Gäste wissen es zu schätzen, denn bei aller Faszination für die Vergangenheit und für die Schönheit der Räumlichkeiten suchen sie dort Ruhe und auch Komfort. Für Besucher, die die Originalität abseits neugieriger Blicke bevorzugen, wurde ein altes Mayahaus restauriert, das traditionsgemäß im Schatten der »casa del dueño« stand. Und dem Architekten Salvador Reyes Rios ist es in der Tat gelungen, eine bescheidene Arbeiterbehausung in einen luxuriösen und modernen Aufenthaltsort zu verwandeln.

Les haciendas du Yucatán ont connu un triste sort quand la production de l' «or vert» a quasiment cessé. Nombre de ces bâtiments grandioses sont tombés en ruines. Ici et là, au-delà d'un portail orné d'arches mauresques, le visiteur distingue les vestiges rongés de ce qui fut autrefois un véritable palais. Dans le cas de la Hacienda San José, située sur la route qui relie Mérida à Tekantó, le regard étonné et ravi s'attarde sur une demeure qui vient de retrouver sa beauté d'antan. Restaurée par les Starwood Hotels & Resorts, la construction fait son entrée dans le 21e siècle dotée du confort le plus sophistiqué. Ce qu'apprécient les hôtes qui, bien qu'attirés par le passé et la beauté des lieux, y cherchent aussi la paix et le bien-être. Pour séduire ceux qui recherchent l'originalité loin des regards curieux, une ancienne maison Maya située, comme le veut la tradition, à l'ombre de la «casa del duegno» a été confiée aux soins de l'architecte Salvador Reyes Rios qui a réussi à transformer une pauvre habitation ouvrière en demeure luxueuse et moderne.

LEFT: *Under the cool awning of the patio, guests can choose to linger over breakfast or while away the hours in a hammock.*
FACING PAGE: *This shady retreat is built of natural materials such as wood and bamboo.*
FOLLOWING PAGES: *Everything has been arranged for maximum comfort and well-being.*

LINKS: *Unter dem Wetterdach des Patios können die Gäste ein Frühstück einnehmen oder sich in einer Hängematte ausruhen.*
RECHTE SEITE: *Mit den Naturbaustoffen Holz und Bambus wurde ein kühlender, Schatten spendender Sonnenschutz errichtet.*
FOLGENDE DOPPEL-SEITE: *Alles ist auf Bequemlichkeit und Wohlbefinden der Gäste ausgerichtet. Nur ein paar Schritte sind es vom großzügig bemessenen Divan zur Freiluftbadewanne.*

A GAUCHE: *Les hôtes peuvent prendre leur petit-déjeuner ou se reposer dans un hamac sous l'auvent du patio.*
PAGE DE DROITE: *Cet abri frais et ombragé est construit en matériaux naturels, bois et bambou.*
DOUBLE PAGE SUI-VANTE: *Tout est prévu pour le confort et le bien-être des hôtes. Quelques pas seulement séparent le divan aux proportions généreuses de la baignoire en plein air.*

FACING PAGE: *Salvador Reyes Rios has avoided the pitfalls of "faux rustique" in the hacienda interiors, preferring pure, clean lines and minimalist décor. The bathroom is a striking example of understated design.*

RIGHT: *An impressive king-size bed is suspended from the ceiling on thick hemp ropes. This luxury cradle is guaranteed to rock you sweetly to sleep!*

LINKE SEITE: *Der Versuchung »vermeintlicher Rustikalität« hat der Architekt widerstanden. Die einfachen Formen und die sachliche Gestaltung des Badezimmers lassen seine Neigung zum Minimalismus erkennen.*

RECHTS: *Das stabile Kingsize-Bett ist mit starken Hanfseilen in der Decke verankert. Das sanfte Wiegen wirkt Schlaf fördernd.*

PAGE DE GAUCHE: *L'architecte a su rester sourd aux sirènes du «faux rustique». La simplicité des formes et la décoration dépouillée de la salle de bains montrent son penchant pour le minimalisme.*

A DROITE: *Le robuste lit «king size» est suspendu au plafond par de grosses cordes de chanvre. Le doux bercement est propice au sommeil.*

IGRE DEL MAR

Gian Franco Brignone

Costa Careyes

According to Gian Franco Brignone, laying hands on a piece of the Earth is a violation – "so when you violate, do so with care!" Before embarking upon his great works, the respectful visionary knelt humbly upon the ground and asked the Earth's permission to cover it with the splendid buildings he saw in his mind's eye. Brignone, known as "the saviour of Careyes", has worked in close collaboration with his brother Marco and the architects Marco Aldaco, Gilbert Trigano, Diego Villaseñor and Jean-Claude Galibert, enriching this unique collection of coves, rocks and beaches with five spectacular villas dedicated to the five senses. The latest in the series, the "Tigre del Mar", is perched on a clifftop, its wild elegance merging with the natural beauty of its surroundings. The Sea Tiger's faded blue façade, sculpted coral-coloured trees, snow-white interiors and beautiful library with a long ladder leant against the façade "to encourage celestial spirits to roam up and down" embodies its creator's respect of nature and love of beauty.

LEFT: *This spectacular residence stands like a gleaming white fortress, perched above red rock-faces and the glittering coastline of Careyes.*
FOLLOWING PAGES: *The spacious terrace at Tigre del Mar makes a cool and comfortable haven, offering guests the chance to recline on adobe benches beneath a wooden canopy.*

LINKS: *Wie eine weiße Festung überragt das Haus die rötlichen Felsen und die Küste von Careyes.*
FOLGENDE DOPPELSEITE: *Die große Terrasse von Tigre del Mar mit Bänken aus Adobe und einem Wetterdach aus Holz verspricht Kühle und Behaglichkeit.*

A GAUCHE: *Telle une forteresse blanche, la demeure domine les rochers rougeâtres et la côte de Careyes.*
DOUBLE PAGE SUIVANTE: *Sur la vaste terrasse de Tigre del Mar, des bancs en adobe et un auvent de bois offrent fraîcheur et confort.*

Sich einen Teil der Erde anzueignen, bedeutet für Gian Franco Brignone, ihr Gewalt anzutun, und »wenn man ihr schon Gewalt antut, dann muss man es wenigstens richtig machen!« So hat sich der große Visionär von Careyes vor Beginn der Arbeiten demütig hingekniet und die Erde um die Erlaubnis gebeten, sie mit seinen Gebäuden zu bedecken. Seither gilt er als »Retter von Careyes«. Mithilfe seines Bruders Marco und Architekten wie Marco Aldaco, Gilbert Trigano, Diego Villaseñor und Jean-Claude Galibert hat er diese weltweit einzigartige Flucht von Buchten, Stränden und Klippen um fünf spektakuläre Villen bereichert, die den fünf Sinnen gewidmet sind. Die Letzterbaute heißt »Tigre del Mar«; sie erstrahlt auf dem Gipfel einer Klippe in all ihrer wilden Schönheit. Mit einer Fassade in verwaschenem Blau, korallenfarbenen Baumskulpturen, einem schneeweißen Innenleben und einer großen Bibliothek, an der eine lange Leiter »die himmlischen Geister zum Auf- und Absteigen ermuntert«, zeugt das Bauwerk vom Erfolgsstreben, der Achtung vor der Natur und der Liebe zur Schönheit seines Schöpfers.

Pour Gian Franco Brignone, s'emparer d'un morceau de la planète c'est violer celle-ci et «quand on viole, on doit violer bien!». Avant d'entamer ses travaux, le grand visionnaire de Careyes s'est agenouillé humblement et a demandé à la terre l'autorisation de la couvrir de bâtiments nés de son imagination. Depuis, il est devenu le «sauveur de Careyes». Avec l'aide de son frère Marco et des architectes Marco Aldaco, Gilbert Trigano, Diego Villaseñor et Jean-Claude Galibert, il a enrichi cet enchaînement de baies, de plages et de rochers unique au monde de cinq villas spectaculaires dédiées aux cinq sens. Son dernier né, le «Tigre del Mar», rugit au sommet d'une falaise et resplendit de toute sa beauté sauvage. Avec sa façade d'un bleu délavé, ses arbres sculptés couleur corail, ses intérieurs blancs comme neige et sa bibliothèque à laquelle est appuyée une longue échelle «pour encourager les esprits célestes à monter et à descendre», il incarne la volonté de réussir, le respect de la nature et l'amour de la beauté de son créateur.

ABOVE: *Beneath a gigantic palapa and an elegant tower a shimmering blue swimming pool stretches away towards the ocean.*

RIGHT: *A tropical creeper, artistically entwined around one of the palapa's supporting trunks.*

FACING PAGE: *Leaning against a cerulean blue wall in the library, this tapering ladder with its worn wooden rungs bleached by the elements is supposed to attract celestial spirits and beings from other worlds.*

OBEN: *Vor einem trutzenden Turm und einer großzügig dimensionierten Palapa erstreckt sich der Swimmingpool zum Meer hin.*

RECHTS: *Auf einer Stütze der Palapa rankt sich das Muster einer Liane.*

RECHTE SEITE: *Gegen die leuchtend blaue Wand der Bibliothek wurde eine riesige, ausgebleichte Leiter gelehnt, die Geister, möglicherweise aber auch Außerirdische, anziehen soll.*

CI-DESSUS: *La piscine s'étend vers la mer au pied d'une tour digne de Mélisande et d'une palapa aux dimensions généreuses.*

A DROITE: *Le beau dessin d'une liane sur un des troncs supportant la palapa.*

PAGE DE DROITE: *Adossée au mur bleu vif de la bibliothèque, une très haute échelle en bois blanchi par les éléments est censée attirer les esprits et (éventuellement) les extra-terrestres.*

PREVIOUS PAGES:
With its instant evocation of the sea and the sky, blue is one of Gian Franco Brignone's favourite colours.
RIGHT*: The giant palapa forms a protective canopy, shielding the yellow house from the sun. This natural shelter is formed of thick creeper-entwined tree trunks, reaching up to support a conical roof covered with dried palm leaves.*

VORHERGEHENDE DOPPELSEITE:
Gian Franco Brignone liebt Blau, die Farbe des Himmels und des Meeres.
RECHTS*: Unter der riesigen Palapa ist das gelbe Haus vor der Sonne geschützt. Die Baumstämme, um die sich mächtige Lianen ranken, tragen eine kegelförmige Haube, die mit getrockneten Palmzweigen gedeckt ist.*

DOUBLE PAGE PRECEDENTE: *Gian Franco Brignone adore le bleu, couleur du ciel et de la mer.*
A DROITE: *La maison jaune s'abrite du soleil sous la gigantesque palapa. Les troncs d'arbre qu'enlacent de grosses lianes supportent un chapeau conique recouvert de branches de palmier séchées.*

ABOVE AND RIGHT: an original "rest corner" in the open entranceway.
FACING PAGE: The walls of the open-air living room are a vibrant shade of yellow. The African sculptures of water-bearers date from the 1950s.
FOLLOWING PAGES: In the entrance hall a banister painted in watery blue trompe-l'œil ascends to the upper floor. The polished stucco steps of the staircase are painted in yellow to harmonise with the walls. Upstairs the staircase takes on the texture and colour of stone.

OBEN UND RECHTS: eine außergewöhnliche Ruhezone im offenen Eingangsbereich.
RECHTE SEITE: Knallgelb sind die Wände des Freiluftsalons. Die afrikanischen Wasserträgerinnen stammen aus den 1950er Jahren.
FOLGENDE DOPPEL-SEITE: Aus der Eingangshalle weist ein Trompe-l'œil-Handlauf in den oberen Stock. Die Treppenstufen aus poliertem Gips sind farblich auf die Mauern abgestimmt. Oben passt sich die Treppe der Farbe und Struktur des Steins an.

CI-DESSUS ET A DROITE: dans l'entrée ouverte un coin repos inhabituel.
PAGE DE DROITE: jaune vif les murs du salon en plein air. Les porteuses d'eau africaines datant des années 1950.
DOUBLE PAGE SUI-VANTE: Dans le hall d'entrée, une rampe d'escalier peinte en trompe-l'œil s'élance vers l'étage supérieur. Les marches en stuc poli s'harmonisent avec les murs. A l'étage, la palette change de nuances et l'escalier imite la couleur et la structure de la pierre.

SOL DE ORIENTE

Costa Careyes

Sol de Oriente and Sol de Occidente, the twin houses Gian Franco Brignone built in collaboration with the architect Jean-Claude Galibert, stand on opposite sides of Angel Bay in Careyes. The vividly coloured façades of these superb residences, perched atop the rocks, stand out against the turquoise sky, forming a stunning image on one of Mexico's most beautiful coasts. Sol de Oriente, resplendent in tones of rich red ochre, is managed by Gian Franco's son, Giorgio Brignone, who defends Careyes with the same passion as his father. The colour of this spacious house's façade was inspired by the flamboyant sunsets guests marvel at from the veranda each night, savouring a margarita or a glass of champagne. Sol de Oriente (and Sol de Occidente) can be rented for private use, together with the services of an impeccable and courteous staff who do their utmost to make your stay unforgettable. Sol de Oriente's charms are reserved for those who can afford the extravagant bill that goes with such luxurious surroundings. But, after all, the experience is priceless!

PREVIOUS PAGES: *The swimming pool offers breathtaking views, looking out across the rocks and appearing to melt into the turquoise waters below.*
LEFT: *Lush green vegetation and a vivid red wall are framed in a kitchen window with its decorative lattice.*

VORHERGEHENDE DOPPELSEITE: *Der Swimmingpool über den Felsen und dem Meer scheint in den Horizont überzugehen.*
LINKS: *Am Küchenfenster, das mit einem dekorativen Gitter versehen ist, gewinnt man einen kleinen Eindruck von der Fülle der Vegetation hinter der leuchtend roten Mauer.*

DOUBLE PAGE PRECEDENTE: *La piscine domine les rochers et la mer, dans laquelle elle semble se prolonger jusqu'à l'horizon.*
A GAUCHE: *D'une fenêtre de la cuisine ornée d'un claustra, on devine la présence de la végétation luxuriante et d'un mur rouge vif.*

Sol de Oriente und Sol de Occidente, die beiden Häuser, die Gian Franco Brignone in Zusammenarbeit mit dem Architekten Jean-Claude Galibert bauen ließ, liegen zu beiden Seiten der Angel Bay in Careyes einander gegenüber. Hoch auf den Felsengipfeln an einer der schönsten Küsten Mexikos zeichnet sich dieses Zwillingspaar mit seinen leuchtenden Farben vor dem türkisblauen Himmel ab. Verwaltet wird es von Giorgio Brignone, Gian Francos Sohn, der sich ebenso leidenschaftlich wie sein Vater für die Interessen von Careyes einsetzt. Sol de Oriente besticht mit seinen rötlichen Ockertönen, der Farbe des unvergesslichen Sonnenuntergangs, den die Mieter der geräumigen Villa abends bei einem Glas Margarita oder Champagner bewundern können. In Sol de Oriente (wie auch in Sol de Occidente) kann man sich nämlich einmieten, dazu gehört der perfekte Service des höflichen und freundlichen Personals, das alles für einen angenehmen Aufenthalt der wenigen Auserwählten tut, die es sich leisten können, eine sagenhafte Rechnung zu begleichen. Gleichwohl: Sol de Oriente ist ein Traumort – und Träume haben bekanntlich ihren Preis.

A dog shelters from the sun, lounging in the cool shade of the palapa. A stone staircase ascends to the panoramic terrace.

Der kleine Hund bleibt lieber im Schatten der Palapa. Oberhalb der Steintreppe liegt die Panoramaterrasse.

Le petit chien préfère rester à l'ombre de la palapa. En haut de l'escalier en pierre se trouve la terrasse panoramique.

Sol de Oriente et Sol de Occidente, les deux maisons que Gian Franco Brignone a fait construire avec la participation de l'architecte Jean-Claude Galibert, se font face de part et d'autre de la Angel Bay à Careyes. Ces magnifiques jumelles aux vives couleurs, perchées au sommet des rochers, se découpent sur le ciel turquoise d'une des plus belles côtes du Mexique. Gérée par Giorgio Brignone, le fils de Gian Franco, qui défend les intérêts de Careyes avec la même passion que son père, Sol de Oriente séduit par ses teintes d'ocre rouge, couleur de l'inoubliable coucher de soleil que les locataires de cette vaste demeure peuvent admirer chaque soir, une verre de «margarita» ou de champagne à la main. Il est en effet possible de louer Sol de Oriente (et Sol de Occidente), ainsi que le service inégalé d'un personnel courtois et souriant qui fait tout pour rendre agréable le séjour des quelques élus qui peuvent se permettre le luxe de régler une note mirobolante. Mais qu'importe, Sol de Oriente est un endroit de rêve, et les rêves, comme chacun sait, ont leur prix.

The staircase leading to the upper floor and the palapa's conical roof has been colourwashed, diluted red pigment daubed on with a simple sponge technique.

Am Treppenaufgang zum Obergeschoss und zur großen Palapahaube wurde eine Rotpigmentlösung mit einem Schwamm aufgetragen.

La cage de l'escalier qui mène à l'étage supérieur et au grand chapeau de la palapa a été badigeonnée de peinture au pigment rouge diluée et appliquée à l'éponge.

LEFT: *The yellow, curved walls of the passageway open out onto the garden and the pool.*
FACING PAGE: *The latticed canopy above the benches and tables on the terrace casts geometric patterns on the sunflower yellow walls.*
FOLLOWING PAGES: *Piles of yellow pillows and green silk cushions strewn across the banquettes contrast with the red-orange walls behind. Mexico comes alive in a vibrant tapestry of colours!*

LINKS: *Der Durchgang zwischen den geschwungenen gelben Mauern führt in den Garten und zum Swimmingpool.*
RECHTE SEITE: *Ein Wetterdach, das Bänke und Tische schützt, zeichnet geometrische Muster auf die sonnenblumengelben Wände der Terrasse.*
FOLGENDE DOPPELSEITE: *Die Bänke sind mit gelben Sitzpolstern und grünen Kissen aus Seide belegt, die einen Kontrast zu den orangeroten Wänden bilden – Mexiko schillert in vielen Farben.*

A GAUCHE: *Le passage entre les murs jaunes incurvés donne sur le jardin et la piscine.*
PAGE DE DROITE: *L'auvent qui abrite des bancs et des tables dessine des motifs géométriques sur les murs jaune tournesol de la terrasse.*
DOUBLE PAGE SUIVANTE: *Sur les banquettes s'amoncellent des coussins jaunes et des coussins de soie verte contrastant avec les murs rouge orangé – le Mexique vibre de couleurs.*

FACING PAGE: *The caretaker's dogs scamper down the main staircase to greet guests.*
ABOVE: *In the romantic rotunda looking out across the sea, the seats espouse the voluptuous curves of the wall. In accordance with local tradition, the floor is encrusted with pebbles.*
RIGHT: *Exhibited in an alcove in the dining room, these colourful carved wooden masks have been collected from different regions of Mexico.*

LINKE SEITE: *Die Hunde des Hausmeisters empfangen die Besucher auf den Stufen der großen Treppe.*
OBEN: *Die Sitzbänke in der zum Meer gelegenen Rotunde passen sich der Krümmung der Mauern an. In den Boden sind nach hiesiger Tradition kleine Kieselsteine eingelassen.*
RECHTS: *In einer Nische des Esszimmers wurden farbige Holzmasken aus allen Regionen Mexikos angeordnet.*

PAGE DE GAUCHE: *Les chiens du gardien accueillent les visiteurs sur les marches du grand escalier.*
CI-DESSUS: *Dans la rotonde qui fait face à la mer, les sièges épousent l'incurvation des murs. Le sol, tradition oblige, est incrusté de petits galets.*
A DROITE: *Disposés dans une niche de la salle à manger, des masques en bois sculpté polychrome, originaires de toutes les régions du Mexique.*

ASI CASA
Barbara & Maurizio Berger
Costa Careyes

"The first time I saw Careyes it brought tears to my eyes", says Barbara Berger. Such a reaction is understandable, especially when Barbara leads you out onto a huge balcony with sweeping views of the Pacific. This is just one of the design highlights of her spacious apartment in the stunning Casitas de Las Flores complex. The "casitas", built by Gian Franco Brignone in collaboration with architects Alberto Mazzoni and Jean-Claude Galibert, seem to be clinging to the rocks above Playa Rosa. With their brightly painted façades and balconies hung with lush bougainvillea, the "casitas" form a refreshing patchwork of colour. And this palette is in perfect keeping with Barbara's original taste and her passion for bringing different styles together under one roof. Her home, resplendent with the multi-coloured hues of an exotic bird, incorporates an antique door from Rajastan, embroidered Indian fabrics, traditional Mexican furniture and an array of folk curios, which make Casi Casa a veritable feast for the eyes.

PREVIOUS PAGES: *Barbara and Maurizio Berger like to enjoy their breakfast on this balcony, looking out over the sea. And who can blame them when the view – and the private beach below – is as heavenly as this?*
LEFT: *This adobe bench invites those back from a morning stroll to rest their weary limbs.*

VORHERGEHENDE DOPPELSEITE: *Barbara und Maurizio Berger frühstücken auf dem zum Meer gelegenen Balkon. Privatstrand und Ausblick sind einfach paradiesisch.*
LINKS: *Eine Bank aus Adobe lädt müde Spaziergänger zum Ausruhen ein.*

DOUBLE PAGE PRE-CEDENTE: *Barbara et Maurizio Berger prennent leur petit-déjeuner sur ce balcon donnant sur la mer. La plage privée et la vue sont tout simplement paradisiaques.*
A GAUCHE: *Un banc en adobe invite au repos les promeneurs fatigués.*

»Als ich Careyes zum ersten Mal sah, sind mir die Tränen gekommen«, erzählt Barbara Berger. Man versteht ihre Rührung sofort, vor allem wenn man ihr auf den großen Balkon folgt, der auf den Pazifischen Ozean hinausragt und zu ihrer weitläufigen Wohnung im fantastischen Komplex der Casitas de Las Flores gehört. Die von Gian Franco Brignone mithilfe der Architekten Alberto Mazzoni und Jean-Claude Galibert erbauten »casitas« schmiegen sich an den Fels, der die Playa Rosa überragt. Ihre in leuchtenden Farben getünchten Fassaden und die üppigen Bougainvilleen der Balkone wirken wie ein erfrischendes Patchwork. Die Farbpalette dieser Wohnanlage entsprach ganz Barbaras außergewöhnlichem Geschmack und ihrer Vorliebe für einen Stilmix. In dieser Wohnung, bunt wie ein exotischer Vogel, finden sich eine alte Tür aus Rajasthan, bestickte Tücher aus Indien, traditionelle mexikanische Möbel und eine Fülle folkloristischer Nippsachen, die die Casi Casa zu einer wahren Augenweide machen.

Flamboyant pots of bougainvillea decorate the staircase, adding strident splashes of colour to the décor.

An einer Treppenwindung fällt der Blick auf eine der zahlreichen Topfbougainvilleen.

Au détour d'un escalier, le regard s'attarde sur l'une des nombreuses bougainvillées en pots.

«La première fois que j'ai vu Careyes, j'ai pleuré à chaudes larmes», s'exclame Barbara Berger. On comprend facilement son émotion, surtout quand elle vous entraîne sur ce grand balcon qui surplombe l'océan Pacifique et qui fait partie de son vaste appartement dans le complexe sensationnel de Casitas de Las Flores. Construites par Gian Franco Brignone avec l'aide des architectes Alberto Mazzoni et Jean-Claude Galibert, les «casitas» semblent s'accrocher au rocher qui surplombe la Playa Rosa. Avec leurs façades aux couleurs flamboyantes et leurs balcons dissimulés sous des bougainvillées luxuriantes, elles forment un patchwork d'une fraîcheur incomparable. La palette de l'ensemble convenait parfaitement au goût inhabituel de Barbara et à sa prédilection pour les mariages de styles les plus divers. Dans cette habitation bariolée comme un oiseau exotique, on trouve une ancienne porte du Rajasthan, des tissus brodés indiens, des meubles traditionnels mexicains et une foule de bibelots folkloriques qui font de Casi Casa une véritable fête pour l'œil.

The bold colours of the "casitas" reflect Mexico's vibrant palette.

In den Farben der »casitas« spiegelt sich die schillernde Farbpalette Mexikos.

Les couleurs des «casitas» reflètent parfaitement la palette chatoyante du Mexique.

RIGHT: *The beauty of the fabrics covering the traditional "chaises longues" on the terrace is further enhanced by the Mexican pink walls. The scallop shells encrusted in the walls make original candleholders.*

FOLLOWING PAGES: *Barbara's décor revolves around eye-catching objects that dazzle and surprise. This mask embroidered with tiny multi-coloured beads was made by craftsmen in the Oaxaca region. The sumptuous array of embroidered fabrics was gleaned in the course of Barbara's travels.*

RECHTS: *Auf der Terrasse unterstreicht das mexikanische Rosa die Schönheit der Stoffe, mit denen die traditionellen Chaiselongues bedeckt sind. In die Wände eingelassene Jakobsmuscheln bilden originelle Kerzenhalter.*

FOLGENDE DOPPELSEITE: *Barbara hat ein Faible für Blickfänge: Davon zeugen die bestickten Stoffe, die sie von ihren Reisen mitbringt, sowie die mit kleinen bunten Perlen bestickte Maske aus der Region Oaxaca.*

A DROITE: *Sur la terrasse, le rose mexicain accentue la beauté des tissus qui recouvrent les chaises longues traditionnelles. Des coquilles Saint-Jacques incrustées dans le mur sont des porte-bougies originaux et amusants.*

DOUBLE PAGE SUIVANTE: *Barbara adore les objets qui attirent le regard, en témoignent ce masque brodé de petites perles multicolores créé par des artisans de la région de Oaxaca, et les tissus brodés qu'elle rapporte de ses voyages.*

FACING PAGE: *On the guestrooom balcony, the "Calavera Catrina", looks down upon a cushion from Guatemala.*

ABOVE AND RIGHT: *The bold rainbow hues of the fabrics on the terrace make an arresting sight. A sumptuous banquette stands beneath a window from Rajastan.*

FOLLOWING PAGES: *The Bergers have gone for a creative and adventurous colour scheme. The painted terracotta mermaid is one of the highlights of the couple's extensive collection of statuettes made by local Mexican craftsmen.*

LINKE SEITE: *Auf dem Balkon eines Gästezimmers überragt die dunkle Gestalt einer Calavera Catrina ein Kissen aus Guatemala.*

OBEN UND RECHTS: *Auf der Terrasse begeistern die bunten Stoffe. Hinter einer riesigen Liege beeindruckt das Fenster aus Rajasthan.*

FOLGENDE DOPPELSEITE: *Vor Farben haben die Bergers keine Angst. Die kleine Sirenenfigur aus Terrakotta gehört zu einer umfangreichen Sammlung von Statuetten mexikanischer Kunsthandwerker.*

PAGE DE GAUCHE: *Sur le balcon d'une chambre d'amis, la Calavera Catrina domine sombrement un coussin déniché au Guatemala.*

CI-DESSUS ET A DROITE: *Sur la terrasse, les tissus bigarrés enchantent le visiteur. Une fenêtre du Rajasthan domine une immense banquette.*

DOUBLE PAGE SUIVANTE: *Les Berger n'ont pas froid aux yeux quand il s'agit de choisir des couleurs. La petite sirène en terre cuite peinte fait partie d'une vaste collection de statuettes réalisées par des artisans mexicains.*

ABOVE AND RIGHT:
*A semi-circular alcove,
painted in vivid eye-
catching pink, stands
above the bed in one
of the guest rooms. A
similar alcove crops up
again above one of the
benches on the terrace,
showcasing a decorative
straw hat belonging to
the mistress of the house.*
FACING PAGE: *Mex-
ican artisans often
choose to depict scenes
from daily life in their
richly coloured works.*

OBEN UND RECHTS:
*Eine leuchtend rosa aus-
gemalte halbkreisförmi-
ge Nische krönt das Bett
in einem Gästezimmer.
Das Gegenstück dazu
findet sich über einer
Bank auf der Terrasse
und die Hausherrin hat
darin einen ihrer vielen
Strohhüte aufgehängt.*
RECHTE SEITE: *Die
mexikanischen Künstler
stellen in ihren farben-
prächtigen Werken gern
Szenen aus dem Alltags-
leben dar.*

**CI-DESSUS ET A
DROITE:** *Une niche
semi-circulaire, peinte
en rose vif, couronne
le lit d'une chambre
d'amis. On la retrouve
au-dessus d'un banc
de la terrasse où elle
accueille un des nom-
breux chapeaux de
paille de la maîtresse
de maison.*
PAGE DE DROITE:
*Les artisans mexicains
aiment représenter les
scènes de la vie quoti-
dienne dans des œuvres
aux riches couleurs.*

M I OJO

Costa Careyes

In 1968, the Italian banker Gian Franco Brignone flew over the west coast of Mexico and discovered Careyes (named after the Carey tortoises that come to lay their eggs in the region). It was love at first exceptional sight. Describing the spectacular beauty of Careyes is a near impossible task; words are unable to convey the magic of these tranquil turquoise waters, majestic rocks and enchanting natural vistas. Seduced by the charms of Careyes, Brignone started out building a modest-sized residence at Careyitos Bay. Then, after constructing a "palapa" house at Playa Rosa and the famous horseshoe-shaped hotel, El Careyes, he began work on Mi Ojo (My Eye). This stunning house, set opposite an islet, was inspired by the loss of Brignone's right eye. And it makes an unforgettable sight, the contrast between the blinding white and electric blue of its façade, the terrace overlooked by a round-eyed window and the flamboyant sunsets remains engraved upon the memories of all those lucky enough to have gained admittance to the magical "theatre of Careyes".

PREVIOUS PAGES: *Coconut palms cast a dappled reflection on the still waters of the geometric-shaped pool.*
LEFT: *A smiling serving girl bearing glasses of Agua de Jamaica (a sweet drink made from crushed hibiscus flowers).*

VORHERGEHENDE DOPPELSEITE: *Die ausgefranste Silhouette einer Gruppe von Kokospalmen spiegelt sich im stillen Wasser des geometrisch angelegten Swimmingpools.*
LINKS: *Ein Hausmädchen bringt lächelnd Gläser mit Agua de Jamaica, einem gezuckerten Sud aus Hibiskusblüten.*

DOUBLE PAGE PRECEDENTE: *La silhouette ébouriffée d'un groupe de cocotiers se reflète dans les eaux calmes de la piscine aux lignes géométriques.*
A GAUCHE: *Une des servantes apporte en souriant des verres remplis d'Agua de Jamaica, une décoction sucrée de fleurs d'hibiscus.*

1968 war der italienische Bankier Gian Franco Brignone mit dem Flugzeug über der mexikanischen Westküste unterwegs, sah die Gegend von Careyes, so genannt wegen der Carey-Schildkröten, die dort ihre Eier ablegen, und verliebte sich in diese außergewöhnliche Landschaft. Die Schönheit von Careyes beschreiben zu wollen, ist verfänglich: Allzu leicht verfällt man dem Zauber türkisblauen Wassers, majestätischer Felsen und eines berückenden Panoramablicks. Schon bald darauf ließ Brignone ein erstes bescheidenes Haus in Careyitos Bay errichten, darauf eine Palapa in Playa Rosa und anschließend das berühmte hufeisenförmige Hotel El Careyes. Der Verlust seines rechten Auges regte ihn zum Bau von Mi Ojo (Mein Auge) an, einem spektakulären Wohnhaus mit Blick auf eine kleine Insel. Dieses Haus lädt wirklich zu lyrischen Höhenflügen ein. Die Kontraste zwischen dem blendenden Weiß und dem leuchtenden Hellblau der Fassade, zwischen der Terrasse, wo ein Fenster in Form eines weit geöffneten Auges den Akzent setzt, und dem flammenden Sonnenuntergang hinterlassen einen bleibenden Eindruck bei allen, die einmal im Bannkreis des »Theaters von Careyes« gestanden haben.

A circular window – the famous "eye" – in one of the guest rooms, glimpsed from the panoramic terrace.

In einem Gästezimmer blickt man durch das Rundfenster – das berühmte »Auge« – auf die Panoramaterrasse.

Au niveau de la terrasse panoramique, une fenêtre circulaire – le fameux «œil» – dans une chambre d'hôtes.

En 1968, le banquier italien Gian Franco Brignone survolait la côte ouest du Mexique et la région de Careyes, ainsi nommée à cause des carets qui viennent y déposer leurs œufs, et il tomba amoureux de ce site exceptionnel. Décrire la beauté de Careyes est un exercice périlleux; on se laisse facilement emporter par la magie des eaux turquoise, les rochers majestueux et le panorama enchanté. Brignone n'a pas tardé à faire construire une première demeure modeste à Careyitos Bay. Puis, après avoir bâti une maison palapa à Playa Rosa et le célèbre hôtel El Careyes en forme de fer à cheval, il a entamé la construction de Mi Ojo, Mon Œil, une maison spectaculaire en face d'un îlot, que lui a inspiré la perte de son œil droit. La demeure, elle aussi, invite aux envolées lyriques. Le contraste entre le blanc aveuglant et le bleu électrique de la façade, entre une terrasse dominée par une fenêtre qui imite un œil écarquillé et le coucher de soleil enflammé, restent gravés dans la mémoire de tous ceux qui sont admis dans le cercle magique du «théâtre de Careyes».

The master bedroom has an original lighting scheme. The sofa is surrounded by woven baskets that gently filter the glow from tiny lamps inside.

Ein Kanapee im Hauptschlafzimmer ist von geflochtenen Körben umringt, unter denen sich Leuchten verbergen.

Dans la chambre maîtresse, un canapé est entouré de paniers tressés qui dissimulent des luminaires.

PREVIOUS PAGES:
Blue is one of Gian Franco Brignone's favourite colours.

ABOVE AND FACING PAGE: *The palm branch roof of the palapa is reflected in the angular pool.*

RIGHT: *The bedroom, with its all-white décor, exudes an atmosphere of perfect calm.*

FOLLOWING PAGES: *The architecture of Mi Ojo is full of symbolism. The round window and the interlacing circles that form part of the stunning wall fresco were inspired by the loss of Brignone's right eye.*

VORHERGEHENDE DOPPELSEITE: *Gian Franco Brignone liebt die Farbe Blau.*

OBEN UND RECHTE SEITE: *Im Schwimmbecken spiegelt sich die riesige Haube der Palapa.*

RECHTS: *Das ganz in Weiß gehaltene Schlafzimmer verbreitet eine fast unwirkliche Stimmung.*

FOLGENDE DOPPELSEITEN: *Die Architektur von Mi Ojo ist symbolträchtig. Das Rundfenster und die Kreise das Wandfreskos erinnern an Brignones Verlust des rechten Auges.*

DOUBLE PAGE PRECEDENTE: *Gian Franco Brignone adore la couleur bleue.*

CI-DESSUS ET PAGE DE DROITE: *La piscine anguleuse reflète l'énorme chapeau de la palapa.*

A DROITE: *ambiance irréelle dans la chambre maîtresse, toute habillée de blanc.*

DOUBLE PAGES SUIVANTES: *L'architecture de Mi Ojo est riche en symboles. La fenêtre ronde et les cercles entrelacés d'une fresque sur le mur évoquent la perte subie par le maître des lieux.*

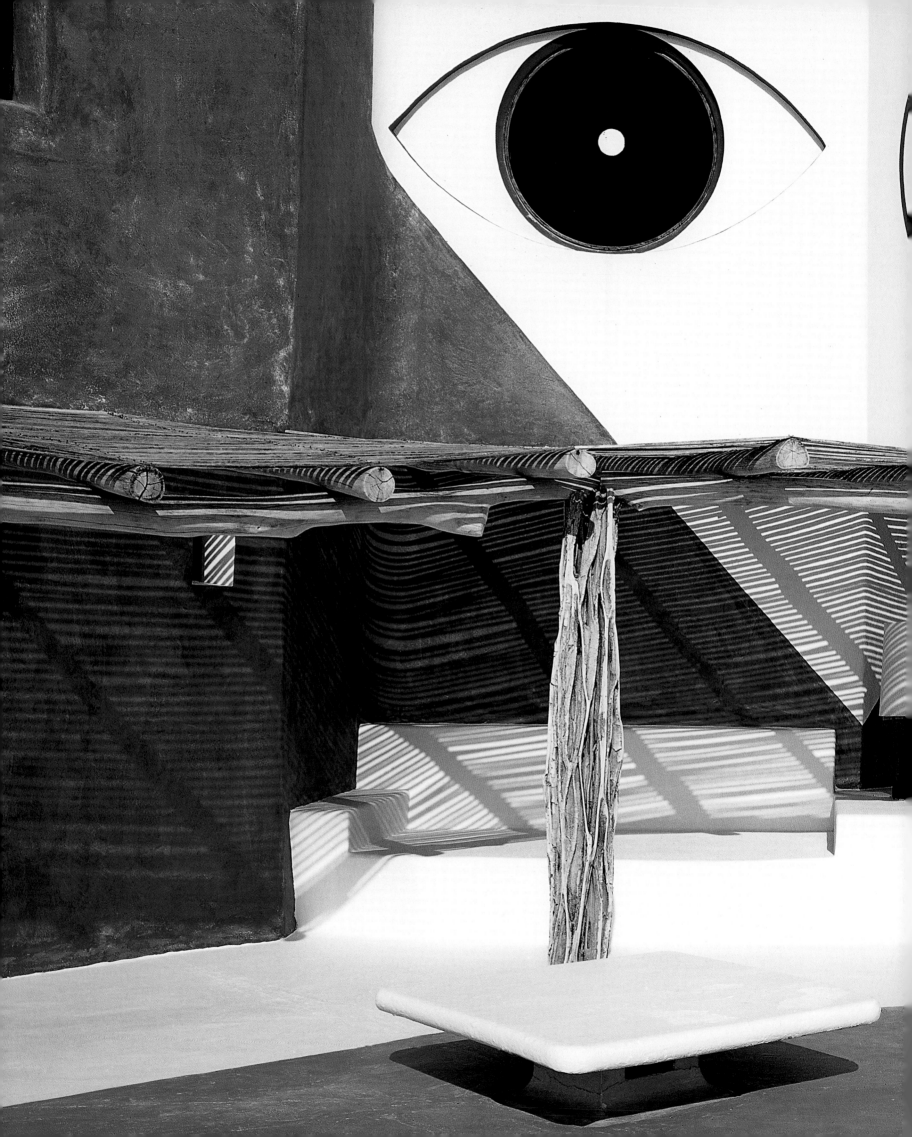

CASA DOS ESTRELLAS

Luciana Paluzzi & Michael Solomon

Costa Careyes

Leaving Manzanillo airport and driving up the coast road towards Puerto Vallarta, the view opens out into vistas of lush vegetation. Groves of coconut palms and banana trees stand out against the azure waters of the Pacific, marking the edge of a mysterious jungle crawling with snakes, scorpions, tarantulas and crocodiles! These exotic surroundings appear to be straight out of a James Bond film. And when you first sight the fortress-like Casa dos Estrellas with its Hollywood-style pool and gigantic palapa, it's easy to believe that you're living the fictional lifestyle of 007. Luciana Paluzzi and Michael Solomon originally came to Careyes on holiday but, seduced by the breathtaking ocean views, they ended up building a spectacular house here complete with clifftop balcony (designed by the renowned architect Manolo Mestre). The mistress of Casa dos Estrellas (the House of Two Stars) is an actress who starred in the James Bond film "Thunderball". Luciana and Michael can certainly pride themselves on owning a sensational home in one of the world's most extraordinary settings.

PREVIOUS PAGES: *Perched on the clifftops like an eagle's nest, the Solomons' spectacular home cuts an impressive fortress-like silhouette.* LEFT: *This breathtaking view from one of the terraces is typical of the stunning vistas in Careyes.*

VORHERGEHENDE DOPPELSEITE: *Adlerhorst, beeindruckende Festung – solche Assoziationen passen auf das Haus der Solomons.* LINKS: *Der Ausblick von einer der Terrassen ist atemberaubend – wie alle Ausblicke in Careyes.*

DOUBLE PAGE PRE-CEDENTE: *Nid d'aigle, forteresse impressionnante – ces termes correspondent parfaitement à la maison des Solomon.* A GAUCHE: *Depuis l'une des terrasses, la vue est époustouflante. Mais toutes les vues le sont à Careyes.*

RIGHT: *Pure, clean architectural lines and vivid rainbow hues.*
FOLLOWING PAGE: *The deep azure blue of the swimming pools reflects the intensity of ocean and sky.*

RECHTS: *Die strenge Architektur in den Farben des Regenbogens.*
FOLGENDE DOPPEL-SEITE: *Das intensive Blau des Pools lässt die Grenzen verschwimmen*

A DROITE: *L'architecture sévère aux couleurs de l'arc-en-ciel.*
DOUBLE PAGE SUIVANTE: *Ici toutes les piscines marient leur bleu intense à celui de la mer et du ciel.*

Wenn man den Flughafen in Manzanillo hinter sich gelassen hat und die Küstenstraße nach Puerto Vallarta entlangfährt, zeigt sich eine beeindruckende Pflanzenwelt: Unzählige Kokospalmen und Bananenstauden trennen die azurblauen Gewässer des Pazifischen Ozeans vom geheimnisvollen Dschungel, in dem Schlangen, Skorpione, Taranteln und Krokodile leben! Der perfekte Schauplatz für einen James-Bond-Film. Bei der Ankunft in der festungsartigen Casa dos Estrellas mit dem Schwimmbad im Hollywoodstil und der riesigen Palapa glaubt man sich tatsächlich in die fiktive Existenz von 007 versetzt. Als Luciana und Michael sich für Careyes als Feriendomizil entschieden hatten, bauten sie sich ein einzigartiges Haus. Der Balkon zum Meer, nach Plänen des berühmten Architekten Manolo Mestre, schmiegt sich an einen Felsen, der eine atemberaubende Landschaft überragt. Da überrascht es nicht mehr, dass die Herrin des »Hauses der zwei Sterne« von Beruf Schauspielerin ist und mit dem James-Bond-Film »Thunderball« Teil der Kinolegende wurde. Jedenfalls können Luciana Paluzzi und Michael Solomon stolz darauf sein, ein Aufsehen erregendes Domizil an einem der außergewöhnlichsten Orte zu besitzen.

Après avoir quitté l'aéroport de Manzanillo et longeant la côte qui monte vers Puerto Vallarta, on est agréablement surpris par la végétation et par les innombrables cocotiers et bananiers qui séparent le Pacifique aux eaux d'azur de la jungle mystérieuse peuplée de serpents, de scorpions, de tarentules et de crocodiles! Un cadre digne d'un film de James Bond. En s'approchant de la Casa dos Estrellas avec son allure de forteresse, sa piscine hollywoodienne et sa palapa démesurée, on est persuadé d'avoir été projeté dans l'existence fictive de 007. Ayant choisi Careyes pour y passer ses vacances, Luciana et Michael se sont construit une demeure sans pareille. Ce balcon sur la mer, bâti d'après les plans du célèbre architecte Manolo Mestre, perché au sommet d'un rocher et qui domine un paysage à couper le souffle. On constatera sans surprise que la maîtresse de la «maison des deux étoiles», actrice de cinéma elle-même, est entrée dans la légende avec «Opération Tonnerre», un film de James Bond. En tout cas, Luciana Paluzzi et Michael Solomon peuvent s'enorgueillir de posséder une demeure sensationnelle dans un des lieux les plus extraordinaires qui soient.

A picturesque path winds down to the private beach.

Eine Treppe windet sich hinunter zum kleinen Privatstrand.

Un escalier sinueux descend vers la petite plage privée.

FACING PAGE: *Beneath the shady palm roof of the palapa, a spiral staircase leads to a tower-top terrace.*
RIGHT: *Bright yellow walls enliven the sunny interior. As you mount the stairs, don't forget to pay your respects to the fish-tailed mermaid on the bas relief.*

LINKE SEITE: *Unter der Palapa führt eine Wendeltreppe auf die Terrasse, die den oberen Abschluss eines Turmes bildet. Eine zeitgenössische Skulptur spiegelt die kräftigen Farben der Bänke und Mauern.*
RECHTS: *Die gelben Wände lassen dieses sonnendurchflutete Interieur erstrahlen. Die Treppe führt an einem Basrelief vorbei, das eine Sirene darstellt.*

PAGE DE GAUCHE: *Sous la palapa, un escalier en colimaçon rejoint la terrasse située au sommet d'une des tours. Une sculpture contemporaine fait écho aux couleurs vives de la banquette et des murs.*
A DROITE: *Les murs jaunes contribuent à égayer cet intérieur ensoleillé. L'escalier passe devant un bas-relief représentant une sirène.*

PLAYA ROSA – CASITAS DE LAS FLORES

Costa Careyes

Can there be anyone who has not fantasised about enjoying their own private corner of paradise somewhere at the ends of the earth? Who has not dreamt of lounging in a secluded, thatch-roofed cabana, surrounded by swaying coconut palms, staring out at a distant horizon where the turquoise ocean merges with an almost unbearably blue sky? Welcome to the world of "dolce far niente", where life is lived with the ocean at your feet and your head in the clouds! Relax in an armchair at the clubhouse, fronting the blissful blue of the Pacific, with a long, cool cock-tail or dine in the gaily coloured restaurant a stone's throw from your door. The lucky inhabitants of the Casitas de Las Flores have access to a private beach – the small but perfectly formed Playa Rosa – via a staircase or a tiny funicular which rocks along at a snail's pace. Down on Playa Rosa, a vibrant pink restaurant, built like a traditional Mayan house, serves delicious regional specialities and freshly caught fish. Is this just a splen-did fantasy? An enticing mirage? Why no, not at all – Costa Careyes is the land where the wildest dreams come true!

PREVIOUS PAGES: *Paradise on earth! Coconut palms wave in the breeze on the private beach at Playa Rosa.*
LEFT: *A pink corridor leading to the garden and the rocks is glimpsed through a narrow open-ing in the back wall.*

VORHERGEHENDE DOPPELSEITE: *Unter den Kokospalmen des Privatstrands von Playa Rosa lässt es sich leben.*
LINKS: *Durch den hohen, schmalen Durch-bruch der Hinterwand blickt man auf den rosa gestrichenen Gang, der zum Garten und zu den Klippen führt.*

DOUBLE PAGE PRE-CEDENTE: *Il fait bon vivre sous les cocotiers de la plage privée de Playa Rosa.*
A GAUCHE: *Une percée haute et étroite dans le mur du fond laisse en-trevoir le couloir peint en rose qui mène au jardin et aux rochers.*

Wer hat nicht schon einmal von einem kleinen Privatparadies am anderen Ende der Welt geträumt, dort, wo Meeres- und Himmelsblau miteinander verschmelzen? Vielleicht in einem von Kokospalmen umgebenen Häuschen mit Strohdach, worin man einen glücklichen Alltag genießen könnte? Wer hat nicht schon dem Wunsch nachgehangen, mit den Füßen im Meer und dem Kopf in den Wolken zu leben und dabei auch noch bequem im Sessel zu sitzen? »Dolce far niente« eben, ein Leben nach Lust und Laune. Mit Blick auf den Pazifischen Ozean, Clubhaus und Longdrink in Reichweite, und einem kleinen Restaurant in fröhlichen Farben quasi vor der Haustür … In Costa Careyes scheinen die tollsten Fantasien und die geheimsten Wünsche mit Leichtigkeit in Erfüllung zu gehen. Die Glücklichen, die in den Casitas de Las Flores wohnen, brauchen nur ein paar Stufen hinabzusteigen oder die kleine, langsame Seilbahn zu nehmen, um zu einem überschaubaren Strand namens Playa Rosa zu gelangen, wo ein Restaurant, das einem historischen Mayabau gleicht, sie mit köstlichen Gerichten und fangfrischem Fisch empfängt. Ein Traum? Eine Fata Morgana? Ganz und gar nicht. In Costa Careyes werden Träume wahr.

Qui de nous n'a pas rêvé d'un coin de paradis privé, quelque part, à l'autre bout du monde, là où la mer et le ciel (d'un bleu si intense qu'il en devient presque insoutenable) se confondent et où une petite cabane à toit de chaume, entourée de cocotiers, abriterait un bonheur quotidien sorti tout droit d'un roman à l'eau de rose, genre Barbara Cartland? Qui de nous n'a pas caressé le désir de vivre sa vie avec la mer à ses pieds, la tête dans les nuages et confortablement blotti dans un fauteuil? Le «dolce far niente» quoi! La douceur de vivre absolue. Avec vue sur l'océan Pacifique, le club-house et un long-drink à portée de la main et le petit restaurant peint en couleurs gaies à deux pas de la porte … A Costa Careyes les fantasmes les plus fous et les désirs les plus secrets semblent se matérialiser avec une aisance alarmante. Les heureux qui habitent les Casitas de Las Flores n'ont qu'à descendre quelques marches ou prendre un petit funiculaire lent comme un escargot pour aboutir jusqu'à la plage, modeste de dimensions, nommée Playa Rosa et où un restaurant qui ressemble à une vieille demeure maya, agréablement peint en rose, les accueille avec des plats succulents et le poisson le plus frais du monde. Un rêve? Un mirage? Pas du tout. Car à Costa Careyes le rêve devient toujours réalité.

LEFT: *The restaurant's rustic décor is enhanced by a palm-leaf palapa roof and bull's-eye windows outlined in vivid pink.*

FACING PAGE: *The pink bar is decorated with natural materials such as tree trunks, pebbles, whalebone and an oversized palapa roof.*

LINKS: *Rosa eingefasste Bullaugen und ein Palapadach unterstreichen den rustikalen Charakter des Restaurants.*

RECHTE SEITE: *Die Bar im schönsten Rosa wurde auf sehr schlichte Weise mit natürlichen Materialien eingerichtet: Baumstämme, Kiesel, Palapa und ein stattlicher Walknochen.*

A GAUCHE: *Des œils-de-bœuf cerclés de rose vif et un toit en palapa accentuent le caractère rustique du restaurant.*

PAGE DE DROITE: *Le bar, rose à souhait, a été sobrement décoré avec des matériaux naturels: troncs d'arbre, galets, palapa et un os de baleine.*

ACKNOWLEDGEMENTS

DANKSAGUNG

REMERCIEMENTS

The friendship and generosity of Barbara and Maurizio Berger, Evelyn Lambert and Marieke and Pierre Baumgartner made work on this book an absolute joy. We would also like to extend our heartfelt thanks to Catalina Corcuera Cabezut from the Casa Museo Luis Barragán, Mexico, the Barragán Foundation, Switzerland, Sarah Sloan from the Museo Robert Brady, the management at the Hotel Mahakua in Colima, Salvador Reyes Rios and Josefina Larrain Lagos, Maestro Victor Manuel Contreras, Chuck and Dev Stern and Nancy Lara at the Hacienda Petac. And last but not least, a big thank you to everyone who showed us such hospitality and kindness throughout our stay.

Dank der Großzügigkeit unserer Freunde Barbara und Maurizio Berger, Evelyn Lambert sowie Marieke und Pierre Baumgartner war die Produktion dieses Buches ein reines Vergnügen. Dank gebührt auch Catalina Corcuera Cabezut von der Casa Museo Luis Barragán in Mexiko, der Barragán Foundation in der Schweiz, Sarah Sloan vom Museo Robert Brady, der Direktion des Mahakua Hotels in Colima, Salvador Reyes Rios und Josefina Larrain Lagos, Maestro Victor Manuel Contreras, Chuck und Dev Stern sowie Nancy Lara von der Hacienda Petac, und natürlich all jenen, die uns mit großer Gastfreundschaft Willkommen geheißen haben.

Grâce à l'amitié et à la générosité de Barbara et Maurizio Berger, Evelyn Lambert et Marieke et Pierre Baumgartner la production de ce livre fut un véritable paradis sur terre. Un grand merci également à Catalina Corcuera Cabezut de la Casa Museo Luis Barragán, Mexique, la Barragán Foundation, Suisse, Sarah Sloan du Museo Robert Brady, la direction de l'hôtel Mahakua à Colima, Salvador Reyes Rios et Josefina Larrain Lagos, Maestro Victor Manuel Contreras, Chuck et Dev Stern et Nancy Lara de la Hacienda Petac et à tous ceux qui nous accueillirent avec une gentilesse et une hospitalité sans égales.

Barbara & René Stoeltie

PAGE 2: *On a path on the Yucatan peninsula, a young boy sells fruit and sweets.*
SEITE 2: *Auf der Halbinsel Yucatán verkauft ein Junge Früchte und Knabbereien.*
PAGE 2: *Sur un petit chemin de la presqu'île du Yucatán, un jeune garçon vend des fruits et des friandises.*

PAGE 4: *Mexican folk art and craftwork in Barbara and Maurizio Berger's Casi Casa.*

SEITE 4: *mexikanisches Kunsthandwerk in Barbara und Maurizio Bergers Casi Casa.*
PAGE 4: *Folklore mexicain dans la Casi Casa de Barbara et Maurizio Berger.*

PAGES 6–7: *the terrace wall of Casa Luis Barragán, painted in vivid Mexican pink.*
SEITE 6–7: *die mexikanisch-rosa getünchte Terrassenmauer der Casa Luis Barragán.*
PAGES 6–7: *le mur de la terrasse peint en rose mexicain de la Casa Luis Barragán.*

To stay informed about upcoming TASCHEN titles, please request our magazine at www.taschen.com or write to TASCHEN, Hohenzollernring 53, D–50672 Cologne, Germany, Fax: +49-221-254919. We will be happy to send you a free copy of our magazine which is filled with information about all of our books.

© 2004 TASCHEN GmbH
Hohenzollernring 53, D–50672 Köln
www.taschen.com

© 2004 for the works by Luis Barragán: Barragán Foundation / VG Bild-Kunst, Bonn

Concept, edited and layout by Angelika Taschen, Berlin
Design by Catinka Keul, Cologne
General project management by Stephanie Bischoff, Cologne
Text editing and coordination by Christiane Blass, Susanne Klinkhamels, Cologne
English translation by Julie Street, Paris
German translation by Stefan Barmann, Cologne

Printed in Germany

ISBN 3–8228–2890–4 (Edition with English/German cover)
ISBN 3–8228–2891–2 (Edition with French cover)

**TASCHEN'S
HOTEL BOOK SERIES**
Edited by Angelika Taschen

"'Decorator porn,' a friend calls it, those sensuous photograph books of beautiful houses. Long on details and atmosphere and packed with ideas, this is a bountiful look at beautiful but unpretentious homes in the place where 'everything is founded on the link between beauty and well-being.' It's easy to linger there."
The Virginian-Pilot, USA

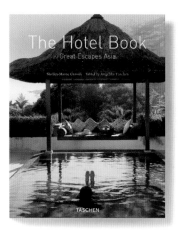
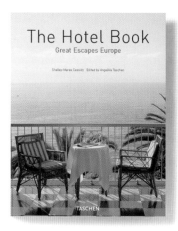

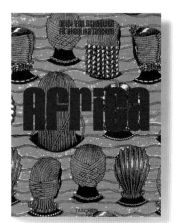

IN PREPARATION:
The Hotel Book
South America

IN PREPARATION:
Inside Asia

**TASCHEN'S
LIVING IN SERIES**
Edited by Angelika Taschen

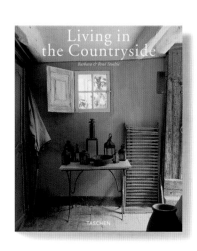
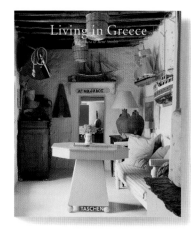
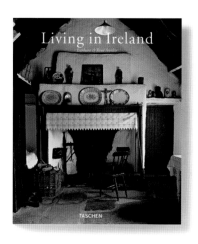
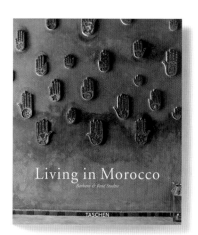

All Spanish/Italian/Portuguese editions